The Barrier and the Bridge
Historic Sicily

The Barrier and the Bridge

Historic Sicily

written and illustrated by
Alfonso Lowe

W. W. Norton & Company, Inc.
New York

FIRST AMERICAN EDITION, 1972

SBN 393 05436 5

72-183655

1968 Marsh. 4-25-74 (Bc.O.)

Printed in Great Britain

Contents

Colour Illustrations

Note The monochrome illustrations are listed in the index.

The author wishes to thank Jocelyn Gibb
for his designing this book and for his
enthusiastic help in seeing it
through the press

Introduction

Prospect from the Mountain of Love

The accident of Sicily's position has to a large extent determined her history. A barrier between the halves of the Mediterranean, she could be vitally important to such eastern nations as depended on the west for essential materials; tin, which transforms soft copper into the hard bronze of the Homeric age, was indispensable for the manufacture of arms and armour, axes and tools. Whoever held Sicily controlled the supply of tin, both from Spain and from Cornwall; hence the long drawn out struggle between Greece and Phoenicia for supremacy in the narrow seas. But Sicily was at the same time a bridge between Europe and Africa; as the tides of conquest ebbed and flowed, Sicily was the springboard, now for European conquests in North Africa, now for the many-pronged oriental design on Europe. Her inhabitants lived in constant peril as long as supremacy in the Mediterranean was in dispute; whenever this was decided they tasted the neglect accorded to a distant appendage and the requisitions of a greedy master. The object of this book is to give a fleeting view of some of the people and events that have moulded Sicily's destiny, and a glance at some of the material treasures they have left us.

An overwritten parchment is called a palimpsest, later writers having tried to erase earlier texts and use the expensive material again. Sometimes the process has been repeated twice, so that the investigator, with his ultra-violet or fluorescent photography, reveals a Latin text under an Arabic manuscript, and a Greek one below that. Sicily offers the same riddle to the interested traveller who can similarly detect the traces of these and many other civilizations in every part. A Norman castle contains portions of a Roman temple, replacing a Greek one built over a Carthaginian sanctuary on the site of the primitive shrine of the earliest inhabitants; in a wall built on Phoenician foundations is an Arabo-Norman gate where the French garrison was slaughtered during the Sicilian Vespers in the thirteenth century; a single mountain top was visited, so we are told, by Hercules, Daedalus and Aeneas, and was captured in turn by Himilco of Carthage, Dionysus of Syracuse, Pyrrhus of Epirus, Romans, Goths, Byzantines, Arabs and Normans, thereafter passing through the hands of a half dozen other nations.

All these examples are taken from the little town of Erice, itself almost an epitome of the history of Sicily. Since the days of the goddess of fertility, for love was only a by-product, variously called Ashtaroth or Astarte, Aphrodite and Venus, when sailors trudged up the steep mountainside with their heavy offerings of wine for the sacred prostitutes of the temple, Erice has captured the imagination. Even Verres, the most rapacious Roman of them all, spared the shrine of Venus Ericina and presented to it a silver statue of Cupid, naturally extorted from elsewhere. Dealing with this, Cicero, whom in our schooldays we regarded as an even greater bore than Thucydides, made one of his rare puns when prosecuting Verres: "I saw the silver Cupid with the lamp," he says. "Is it a symbol of your cupidity?" The story that Verres donated the statue in appreciation of favours received from the temple prostitutes can certainly not be confirmed in Cicero's oration; on the contrary, Verres was busy seducing his hostess, whose family was to bring the trumped-up charge against the reluctant donor.

At Erice you may feel Sicily's every mood, from joyful spring, with its countless varieties of wild flower, to summer, when the prospect of parched, reaped plains keeps alive the legend of a barren, unfriendly land, a legend repeated by every summer tourist who feels the urge to write yet another compendium of misleading information. Here you can experience the sirocco at its worst, howling and buffeting through the narrow streets and tearing up the tallest and oldest trees, while it spares the smaller whose youthful elasticity enables them to bow before the blast. If the sirocco begins on a Friday, say the older natives, it will last for eight days; surely a dim memory of the Moslem day of rest. I have been there when it did indeed begin on a Friday and by Monday all was calm again; but it would take more than a mere fact to negate the fallacy. The sirocco can be more than a nuisance; it has even modified the history of the world. From the south or west you can see the Aegatian Islands on anything but the cloudiest day, the scene of Rome's final victory in the first Punic War and one of the world's decisive battles, when the sirocco immobilized the Carthaginian ships and allowed the Romans, who had the weather gauge, to run alongside and grapple with their newly invented *corvi*, thus converting a sea fight against better seamen into a land battle against an inferior foe.

Autumn, more than any other season, can envelop Erice in cloud so dense that the stranger gropes his way despairingly through the damp, eerie silence; about eighty such days are experienced each year and I wonder whether this could not account for the many times this apparently impregnable stronghold has fallen. I could hardly picture those great walls, against which siege engines could find no foothold on the steep mountainsides, being stormed by an enemy who in clear weather would stand out against the green of spring, the brown of summer or the white of winter's snow.

There is scarcely a feature of Sicily's history which has not left some trace visible on or from the mountain top. It has been claimed, for instance, that Makari, which you can see quite near you to the north-east, is a name of Hittite origin. As the Hittites were not sailors only one possible explanation —always assuming the truth of the claim—occurs to me: looking for the roots of the ancient Minoan civilization of Crete, several authors have suspected a Hittite origin and, quite recently, a strong case has been presented for the decipherment of the oldest Cretan inscriptions in the same language as cuneiform Hittite. Not only were the Cretans noted sailors, and evidence of their seafaring activities goes back to more than 2,000 years before Christ, but they attained special regard throughout the classical world for the inventions of Daedalus, a semi-legendary prototype of the craftsman, cunning of hand and mind. Vincent Cronin has based a fascinating book on the arrival of Daedalus in Sicily, and it was in the temple of Aphrodite of Eryx that Daedalus made his famed offering. A golden honeycomb—the book is so well known that I need not elaborate—was its form. The learned Doctor Pagoto has shown that it was a ram, for somewhere in the long pilgrimage of scholarship a careless scribe wrote "*kerion*" (honeycomb) for "*krion*", and most accepted texts today print the latter; "a golden ram to Aphrodite of Eryx, wonderfully worked and in truth the image of a ram" is the sense of the passage from Diodorus Siculus. Why should one quibble, you may ask, so long as the arch of Daedalus and the bridge of Daedalus are pointed out to the visitor?

The answer conducts you into a maze of folklore more intricate than that which Daedalus himself is said to have built for King Minos of Crete. The mountain was, as I have said, dedicated to the worship of Ashtaroth and dominates the western tip of Sicily, where the first Phoenician colonies were established. In the ancient Semitic languages gods and goddesses were called *bel* and *ishtarat*, or by words derived from the same roots. When a supreme god, whom we would call "God" with a capital G, was to be designated he was likewise called Bel or, in the form more familiar to us, Baal. Even in the Hebrew Old Testament, where the supporters of monotheism waged a perpetual war against the worshippers of the older Canaanite Baal, the Lord is occasionally referred to as Baal, for instance in Hosea ii, 16. Similarly *lshtar*, *ashtaroth* and *hashtarat* are simply common nouns denoting a goddess or goddesses.

Many years ago Skipwith postulated that the primitive pastoral Semites traced their own *and* their flocks' ancestry to a common divine mother, indiscriminately woman or ewe. Thus Rachel, by derivation, becomes "the ewe that makes fruitful" and Rachel-Ephrath, ancestress of Joseph, is the Syrian goddess of moon and flock; among the sons of Lamech is Jabal, or Yabal, Phoenician for "ram" and father of the pastoral clan. The same "*ilu*" or "*el*" figures in Abel, keeper of sheep, and thus, still according to Skipwith, the Semitic word for "god"—*el, ilu* or *allah*—originally had the concrete significance of "ram". In the same way *ishtar* and all its variations are derived from the Semitic root for "ewe". Small wonder, then, that the worship of the goddess of the high places, so abominated by the children of Israel, should be connected with flocks and herds; so the mythical Eryx, on whose mountain we are standing, was the son of Aphrodite and Butes the herdsman, and Aeneas was the son of Aphrodite, the Roman Venus, and Anchises, who was pasturing his flocks on Mount Ida, behind Troy, when the goddess condescended to mate with him. And in this way we come back to the shrine of the universal mother of flocks and men, to whom Daedalus dedicated the most appropriate offering, a golden ram.

Due east you can almost imagine you see the temple of Segesta nestling among the hills, a monument to Greek influence among the Elymians [*Col. pl. I(b)*]. This early race may have come, like the Hittites, from Asia Minor; they have been called Phrygians but they themselves claimed Trojan origin. Note the neatness with which Virgil fitted this belief to Aeneas, his hero and legendary founder of the Roman race. His father Anchises conveniently dies near Trapani on the long voyage from Troy to Italy and is buried at the foot of the mount of Eryx. Trapani is Drepanum, which is a borrowed Greek word for sickle and accurately describes the shape of the harbour; from there it is only a step for Aeneas to the summit of the mountain, where he founds a temple to his mother, as legend credits him with doing in many another spot sacred to the goddess of fertility.

When Aphrodite of Eryx was Ashtaroth of the Phoenicians (and they will be taken to include the Carthaginians), she took an annual holiday in Carthage, in the shape of a red dove or a dove with golden wings, accompanied by a flock of white ones, representing her priestesses, and great was the rejoicing at her return. So in the uninspired religious art of Phoenicia no type was more popular than the goddess or priestess—it is impossible to be more precise—who pressed a dove against her breast. When the Phoenicians departed, the daily sacrifice of a pair of white doves perpetuated the memory and today the city crest includes the same emblem. That the custom of the patroness leaving and returning, the *katagogia* and *anagogia* of Greek times, has not died out, the following tale will witness.

In the late Middle Ages a French ship was threatened with destruction in one of the storms which are so frequent at the western tip of Sicily. Her cargo included a painting of the Virgin, said to have been brought from Egypt, and the safe arrival of the ship in one of the tiny coves north of Trapani was attributed to her intercession, perhaps confused in the turmoil with that of the Madonna of Erice. At all events the pious sailors decided to build her a sanctuary in the harbour, but were dissuaded by the frequency with which the coast was raided by corsairs. Placing the portrait on a bullock cart, therefore, they proceeded inland but the oxen, overcome by fatigue, had barely gone two miles when they lay down and refused to go further. The sanctuary was accordingly built on the spot, now known as the village of Custonaci, and in the church one may see the picture itself, a fourteenth-century painting of the Umbrian school, in its silver aedicula. Not only is this Virgin invoked by the people of Erice in times of drought, but the picture has been carried laboriously on men's shoulders to and from Erice as an annual ceremony. In this way, says Festing Jones, is the *anagogia* of Astarte perpetuated, though since his day the portrait has been declared a national monument and only a copy does the double journey. I suspect that the custom is more widely observed, for the same performance attends the journey of the Virgin of Piazza Vecchia to Piazza Armerina for her annual holiday. We do not of course know the identity of the portrait's owner, nor his reaction on being informed that his property had been so liberally bestowed on a foreign village.

It need not upset us unduly, for Adragna calls the story of the shipwreck a pious legend, designed to wean the superstitious inhabitants from their worship of Aphrodite and celebration of her *anagogia*. He quotes an ecclesiastical document, written in archaic Italian, which states this in so many words and explains the aim of the new festival in honour of Our Lady of Mid-August, and cites the offerings made by pious Christians in place of the tithe of corn that was customarily brought to the goddess of love.

Beyond Custonaci looms the sheer slope of Monte Cofano [*Col. pl. I(a)*] and behind that the promontory of Saint Vitus, a saint much venerated in these parts. His strong point was the cure of certain nervous diseases, especially epilepsy and chorea, popularly called Saint Vitus' Dance, and his emblems are the cock and the dog; the former reminds one of Asklepios, the Greek god of healing, the latter is of special interest, for the saint's miracles include the cure of rabies—a feat which no physician has equalled—and certain nervous spasms, possibly hysterical, called *caninus raptus*, or seizures due to canine possession. It was the hounds of Saint Vitus who came to Erice at the summons of Saint Julian, and there chased the panic-stricken Saracens from the ramparts; the legend may indeed contain a germ of truth, as anyone will admit who has seen a pious Moslem avoiding the ceremonial defilement of a dog's nose. Whatever the truth or explanation may be, the town of Erice changed its name from Gebel Hamed to Monte San Giuliano when the Normans captured it in the eleventh century, and so it remained until Mussolini restored the old name of Eryx in its Italian form.

The last outline on the eastern horizon is the tangle of mountains behind Palermo, among which rises the peak of Montelepre, home of hares—and bandits. Here, a short time ago, Giuliano defied the authorities for seven years, half feared, half revered, at one time an imitation Robin Hood, at another the May Day murderer, whose men fired on a peaceful crowd, presumably with the excuse that they were celebrating a communist holiday, killing seven and wounding thirty-three. Southward again the countryside is open and there, among the prosperous looking farms, lies the last relic of the power of the Mafia; whatever the experts may say about its present scope, the fact that vociferous arguments about it can be heard in bars and other public places suggests that in recent years it has lost much of its silent, sinister threat.

Standing as we are on the north-west corner of Sicily, most of our landmarks have been to the east. To the west, dotted with the chess-board of salt pans, are the flat coastlands and the nearer islands, among which Motya was the first foothold of the Phoenicians, while further south lies Marsala, which conceals their last. Almost at our feet is the port of Trapani, whither an Erycean hostess will despatch one of the family on a motor-cycle to buy a fish or an octopus, on the arrival of an unexpected guest. It was this view that so impressed Samuel ("Erewhon") Butler in 1890 that he decided it must have been the scene where the Odyssey was enacted, and that Trapani was the home of its female author; the work is today more often cited than read. Butler was about fifty-five when he broke a leg and spent two months lying in Erice absorbing local colour. One of his sources of information was Canon Antonino Amico, whom I met shortly before his death at the age of ninety-three and who would talk about his evenings with Samuel Butler seventy years before. It was Amico whose indefatigable research laid the foundation of the excellent library of Erice and discovered so much of the town's history. He had the gift of making the past live, whether through a manuscript record of a sixteenth century outbreak of plague in Erice, or his meetings with the man who penned the immortal phrase "Oh God! Oh Montreal!"

The southern view introduces you to yet another chapter in Sicily's history, the Aragonese and Spanish domination. The first village through which the main road to Marsala passes is called Paceco, more easily recognized in its Spanish spelling of Pacheco, a Spanish family that had its seat here and produced at least one viceroy whose name adorns the Quattro Canti of Palermo. Among the great salt pans, some filled with clear, fresh sea water, some with the half evaporated brown mud and others with the solid residue, looking like anything but salt, stand the windmills which grind the finished product. The history of windmills is intriguing but obscure: they were known in Persia about 2,000 years ago and are believed to have been brought to Europe by the Moslems of Spain: certainly it was the Spaniards who brought them to Sicily. It is usual to dismiss the whole period of Spanish dominance as an unrelieved curse; the windmills of the west coast are only one of the Spanish legacies which make me doubt this. The age of the salt pans is far greater and some authorities regard them as an invention of Minoan or Mycenean times; it has in fact been postulated that the main items of trade in the bronze age were tin, without which there would be no bronze, amber and salt. The last is particularly important to people on a vegetarian diet, the common lot of those who lived where game was scarce and who had no access to the "fishy deep", as Homer called it.

Marsala, in the distance, fills some more gaps in the 3,000 years we are to cover. As Lilybaeum it was the impregnable fortress which defied the Romans for ten years and came to them only by treaty when Carthage lost the first Punic War, at the sea battle of the islands that you see against the western sky, and which I mentioned earlier. Under the Saracens it got its modern name, not from *Marsa Allah*, Harbour of God, as so invariably and incorrectly copied from one author to the next, nor from *Marsa Ali*, but from *Marsa a'la*, the high harbour. The word "high" is of course quite inappropriate to the coastal plain, but *a'la* is commonly used in the sense of superior and there is no doubt that in this respect Marsala scores over Mazara del Vallo, the first Saracen beach-head in Sicily and, as it were, just round the corner. Goethe, in a travel book which could only have sold on the author's name, described Sicily as the key to the whole of Italy; he certainly showed prophetic vision in this instance, for it was at Marsala that Garibaldi was to land with his Thousand, seventy-three years later and, in the most decisive campaign of the Risorgimento, make possible the first united Italy since the fall of the western Roman empire.

All this corner of Sicily is Garibaldi country: southward lie Salemi [*Col. pl. II(a)*], the breath-taking hill town huddled at the skirts of its mother castle, where the liberators spent the first night ashore; and Calatafimi, the first battle in which the red shirts defeated the Neapolitan troops of the Bourbons. Trapani museum contains the authentic uniform of a *garibaldino* and one can admire the stained russet shirt that was once red, the shirt that was parent to so many others, black, brown, grey and blue, and the only one to survive in popular esteem. Its disadvantages in open warfare were neutralized by its very brightness; the first lot, destined for the slaughter-house workers of Buenos Aires, was found in the warehouse of a merchant of Monte Video when Garibaldi, at the head of the Italian Legion, fought for Uruguay against Argentine tyranny. Once the Italians were thus conspicuously clad they could no longer melt away insensibly when the action became too hot. Whether for this reason or from sentiment, Garibaldi's Thousand and the recruits whom they gathered, wore the red shirt until the end of his campaigns. I have mentioned the village of Paceco; did Garibaldi ever remember, when he was in this part of Sicily, that the Uruguayan Minister of War who authorized the establishment of the Italian Legion, was also called Pacheco?*

In 1862 Garibaldi landed again at Palermo to raise troops for a new project, the liberation of Rome from the French troops of Napoleon III. Amid the inconceivable betrayals of the men whom he had established as rulers of Italy, his simple-minded enthusiasm stands out in sharp relief; he was not to know that the king he had made was to have some of his followers killed or that he himself, unresisting, was to be wounded by Italian troops. The people of Sicily, imbued with the same exhilaration, flocked to his standard. In flower-decked Marsala a fisherman's voice was heard above

* The pronunciation is identical, in both Italian and Spanish spelling.

the cheering throng, shouting "*Roma o morte!*", and a few hours later Garibaldi stood before the cathedral altar to swear "Rome or death".

On the island of Motya or San Pantaleo, a link between Sicily's earliest and latest history, stands a bench and above it you may read the stone tablet which tells how he came here to rest in the summer of 1862, after the feverish events of Marsala.* The trip, on a pleasant day, is one which the educated visitor cannot afford to miss, for Motya represents the only readily accessible Punic (by which I designate both Phoenician and Carthaginian) site. When I say "readily", the term must be qualified to allow for holidays, bad weather or bad luck. Having obtained a written permit in Marsala from the genial Colonel Lipari, and it is better to ascertain his whereabouts from any lounger in front of the cathedral rather than to try at his office, the visitor goes five miles north along the coast road; the good colonel will tell you two kilometres, but that is merely to save you being alarmed at the distance to be travelled. Guide books which tell you that you can sail from Marsala to Motya are written by authors who have presumably crossed with a large party. As you go north you pass through a small village, where a crudely painted board directs you down a side street to the left; a deplorable earth road takes you between the salt pans to a shed beside a narrow canal,

***

Qui Giuseppe Garibaldi, dopo proferito il
gran detto in Marsala
ROMA O MORTE
Venne a riposare
il 20 Luglio 1862

To judge by the story books, you would think that Garibaldi was a man of few words, these being invariably "Rome or Death". At any rate, patriotic citizens like to point out a place in more than one town where the famous slogan was uttered; in Cefalù it is on the main street.

and here you must stand on a mound and wave a handkerchief. Theoretically this is observed by an eagle-eyed watcher on the island a mile away and a boat is sent; in practice you go on waving hopefully until the custodian arrives at about 2.30 p.m. to fetch his little daughter home from school. The journey across the shallow lagoon is uneventful, father resting in the shade of the engine housing while his rosy-cheeked daughter stands aft and steers with the tiller between her chubby legs.

The wild flowers of Sicily are a proverb, says Sladen, but nowhere do they attain such profusion as on Motya [*Col. pl. II(b)*]. As you walk along the water's edge, admiring the fine ashlar masonry of the ancient walls between clumps of sisal, agave and prickly pear, you tread a carpet of pimpernel and peavetch, iris and hyacinth, clover and celandine. The last, which has ceased to flower by May, is known to us also by the less attractive name of pilewort for "... made into an oil, ointment or plaister," wrote Culpepper, "it readily cures both the piles, or haemorrhoids, and the king's evil." Assuming that we have no urgent need to pick the lesser celandine, we may stroll north for about 300 yards, when we arrive at the old North Gate [*below left*], whose remains have stood up wonderfully to the wind and rain of two millennia; perhaps the dry summers hereabouts have something to do with it, for no salt industry can survive through summer rains, and the neat, tiled stacks of salt among the drying pans are a guarantee of good weather [*below*].

From the North Gate you can see a projection of the mainland, where the Birgi cemetery has revealed the Punic graves that could no longer be accommodated on an island of 125 acres, for you must realize that Motya was a Phoenician strongpoint from the time of King Solomon; it may in fact

have been founded at the bidding of Hiram of Tyre. A glance at the map shows how, with Carthage, it controls the narrowest part of the Mediterranean, through which Phoenician ships passed to Tarshish or Tartessus, beyond the straits of Gibraltar, since the earliest days. By no means devoid of strategic skill, the Phoenicians planted their colonies with an eye to protecting their lucrative commercial empire in the western Mediterranean. Motya itself would have looked almost impregnable, an island in a sheltered lagoon with ample anchorage for its protecting fleet and sturdy walls that came down to the water's edge. And from where you stand, an easily defended causeway runs from shore to shore, a foot or two below the surface of the lagoon, so well constructed by the Carthaginians that horses and carts still use it at certain times. When Dionysus of Syracuse besieged Motya in 398 B.C., he repaired the causeway which the defenders had partially destroyed, and used it as an emplacement for his siege engines, the first time in the world's history that catapults were used. So well had his tactics been rehearsed that he first defeated the Carthaginian fleet with anti-personnel missiles and then, from the same emplacement, proceeded to batter the island's walls. As usual after a Greek victory, Dionysius supervised an orgy of massacre and enslavement, the former including the three thousand Greeks who had fought on the Carthaginian side. When we come to consider the era of Hellenic civilization in Sicily we shall find the same association of genius, technology, ethics and ideals with a ruthless barbarism which makes the ancient Greeks appear quite modern.

"And he put down the idolatrous priests, whom the kings of Judah had ordained to burn incense in the high places in the cities of Judah, and in the places round about Jerusalem; them also that burned incense unto Baal, to

18

the sun, and to the moon, and to the planets and to all the host of heaven . . .
And he defiled Topheth, which is in the valley of the children of Hinnom,
that no man might make his son or his daughter to pass through the fire to
Moiech . . . And he took away the horses that the kings of Judah had given
to the sun . . . And the high places that were before Jerusalem, which
Solomon the king of Israel had builded for Ashtoreth the abomination of the
Zidonians . . ."

The foregoing is to forestall the smugness with which those who profess
the so-called monotheistic religions discuss the habits of the Carthaginians.
If you read the second Book of Kings you will find that Josiah tried to
eradicate from Jerusalem the very practices which give the Carthaginians
such a bad name. Male and female temple prostitution, the pagan rites on
the high places, the effigy of the horse and palm tree on Carthaginian coins *
[above left], all were a common Semitic heritage. And the children that
were burned alive, usually to appease the gods in times of danger, are found
in the *topheth* of Motya as in Carthage, Sousse and other Phoenician
settlements. Following the coast past the North Gate you soon come to the
sanctuary, where the loose earth is studded with tiny amphorae containing
the bones of children aged from two to twelve. That the custom had been
practised for many years is shown by the same pathetic jars at the bottom of
an excavation fifteen feet in depth [*overleaf*]. We know that the child
victims were selected from the noblest families, for these were expected to

* The Greek word Phoenix means both a Phoenician and a palm tree. The inscription on the
reverse is in late Phoenician script and reads (from right to left) "*Ommachanat*", i.e. "in the
camp" or, as we should say: "On active service". The obverse is simply a copy of the Syracuse
head of Arethusa [*above*].

19

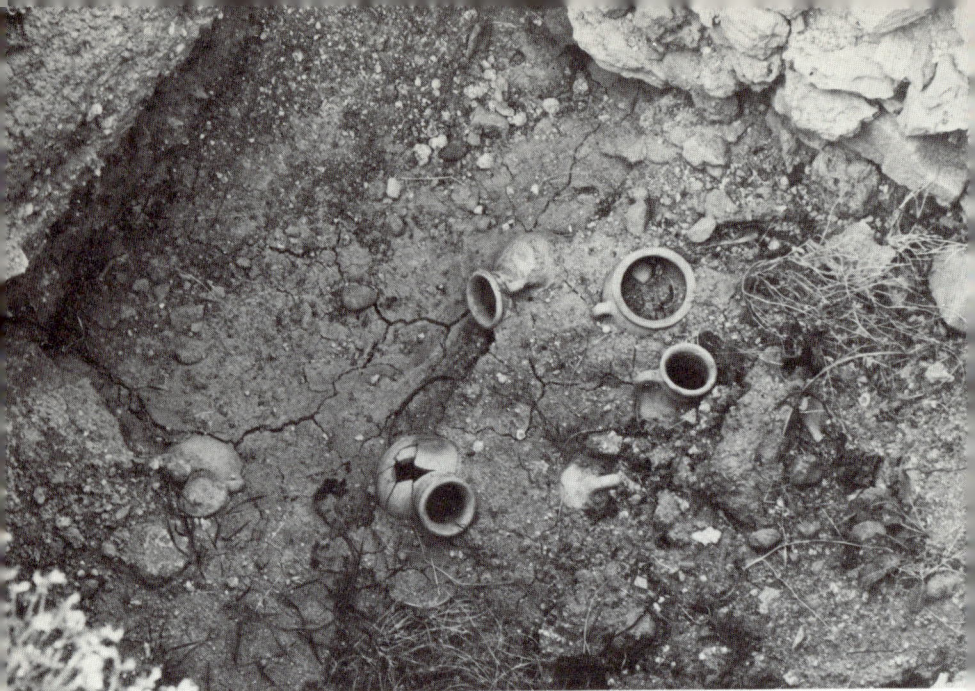

make the greatest sacrifice on the city's behalf; but we also know that, from time to time, the wrath of the gods (not Moloch) was aroused by the substitution of slave children for those of aristocratic birth. I draw attention to Moloch because of the belief, probably derived from Flaubert's book *Salammbô*, that there was a god of that name inside whose brazen statue the children were burned. The sacrifice was, in fact, made to the goddess Tanit and the name Moloch apparently derives from the word *mol'k*, a holocaust.

Walls, watch towers and a tiny inner harbour all remind us of Carthaginian times; the best, however, is to be seen in the museum that houses the finds of Joseph Whitaker, head of the famous house that supplied Nelson with Marsala wine, who performed the miracle of changing, not water into wine, but wine into antiquities. There is the huge, weathered slab of stone portraying two lions on a prostrate bull; Mycenean, say the writers, thinking it safe to follow their leader. But precisely the same motif can be seen on a sixth century Corinthian vase at Agrigento, showing the same oriental influence. The lions making their kill was, in fact, the city crest of Motya and it is more reasonable to derive it directly from the east than from the lost art of Mycene.

What a wealth of history is displayed here! Egyptian scarabs, glass beads and amulets, many of them miniature gods from the Egyptian pantheon which were adopted by the Phoenicians in many parts; the dwarf demi-god Bes was a great favourite and can be seen not only as an ornament but as the

20

remote ancestor of the Toby jug. Delicate glass vases remind us that Syria borrowed the art of glass-making from Egypt and improved on it, that the Byzantines brought it from Syria to Aquileia, at the head of the Adriatic, whence it fled from the threat of barbarian invasions to the Venetian islands, where it still survives, degraded but flourishing, on the island of Murano. Among the coins found on the island and here displayed is an Arabic apothecary's weight of glass, one of many that circulated as money from time to time.

Another Phoenician legacy persists in western Sicily to this day. Here, in the home of Punic power, guarding the narrow passage between Sicily and Carthage, were funerary *stelae* of various patterns, imitating the profusion of such memorials uncovered at Carthage. Several are shaped, or decorated, to represent a simple shrine of the *aedicula* type, and bear symbols such as the crescent and disc of Tanit Pene Baal. Without going too deeply into a still disputed question, it may be assumed that Tanit was a western equivalent of Ashtaroth, and that *pene baal*, meaning face of Baal, the sky god, represents the crescent new moon with the old moon (and the man in the moon) in her arms. The same concept persisted through biblical times and can be found in the Jewish Talmud, a collection of interpretations of the Law committed to writing towards the end of the second century of our era, at the earliest: ". . . welcome the face of their Father which is in Heaven once in the month." The palm tree and the column are said to go back to the primitive belief in the tree spirit, which in our civilization is relegated to the domain of pre-history, until the 25th December.

Now if you examine the so-called *caduceus*, the staff entwined with twin serpents, you will find that in Punic representations it consists of a disc on a beribboned staff, surmounted by a crescent. This also was a symbol of Tanit, but her most popular representation, possibly derived from the Egyptian *ankh*, looks like a child's drawing. Among other representations are the palm tree, usually shown with one or more men climbing up, presumably to perform artificial fertilization, and the open hand, palm forward, then as now a potent amulet and averter of the Evil Eye.

The next step in a strange inheritance will be found in the Archaeological Museum of Palermo, where a whole gallery of tomb *aediculae* from western Sicily are displayed. These have the same shape, the same Carthaginian emblems of Tanit-Baal worship, and a panel in the centre on which a dining-room scene is painted, man reclining, woman sitting and servants replenishing the tables; above the main figures, who are pledging each other, can be read a Greek inscription, such as "MARIA ERUS AGATHA" which might perhaps invoke a tutelary Mary the Good. To read Maria here suggests strongly that these *stelae* date from Christian times, for in the Semitic languages, Mary would surely be written as the original Miriam. If so it is only another example of our conservatism through the ages, for nothing could be more incongruous than a Christian funeral banquet embellished with the symbols of Ashtaroth. The last link in an unbroken chain of 2,500 years can be seen in any roadside shrine. In the neighbourhood of Marsala, *and in no other part of Sicily*, such shrines, with their pictures of the Blessed Virgin, the Saviour, or some locally revered saint, are of exactly the same shape and size as the Phoenician *aediculae*. This is a good example, but not a unique one, of the persistence of tradition in Sicily. We shall meet with others.

Though the authorities are trying to spoil it with stark girders bolted into the shape of radio masts, Erice is still one of the most beautiful and evocative towns of Europe. Nor is it a difficult one for the sightseer for it is small enough to ensure that any of the tortuous lanes will soon open on to a recognizable landmark. I shall therefore conduct you on an imaginary tour without the detailed instructions of a guide book, confident of the impossibility of your getting lost.

The city of Erice occupies the flat top of a rock, whose sides are steep in parts, sheer in others. Its outline is that of an equilateral triangle, the apex pointing north and the Porta Trapani, where we enter, lying at the bottom left-hand corner. This gate, like others that we shall see, is mediaeval in its present form and stands divorced from its walls so as to allow traffic to enter alongside and emerge through the arch. Not that the volume of traffic constitutes a problem, consisting as it does mainly of motor tricycles, hawking fish and other everyday necessities that have been brought from Trapani. The paucity of traffic is peculiar to Erice and strikes the visitor early in his first venture; the scarcity of shops is equally surprising and prepares one for the pervading and unusual quietness that is as distinctive as the city crest and was responsible for d'Annunzio calling Erice "the city of silence". As in an oriental town, the houses face inwards and family life is conducted in the courtyards that are largely survivals of the fourteenth, fifteenth and sixteenth centuries; hence one misses several features of the usual Mediterranean town. No children play in the streets—in any case most of them take the cable car to school in Trapani every day; no washing festoons the streets and in the evening one sees no gossips on the doorsteps and, if it comes to that, very few doorsteps either. The courtyards themselves, if you are lucky enough to be invited in, will impress you with the ancient stone washing troughs whose origins may be lost in antiquity, and with flowers, trees and creepers. Such is the blessed silence that even the town band, accompanying a saint's procession through the narrow streets, sounds extramundane.

The first noteworthy building that you see after the Porta Trapani is the cathedral, with its separate belfry before it [*Col. pl. III*]. The belfry is a few years older than the church, having been built by Frederick of Aragón in 1312, as a watch tower after the War of the Sicilian Vespers. The twin windows, separated by a delicate column, plain or spiral, and surmounted by an arch decorated with various devices, are your first encounter with a typical Sicilian architectural feature that persisted with modifications from Norman to Renaissance times. The cathedral itself is a Gothic building, to which has been added an attractive fifteenth-century porch. In 1856 barbarians masquerading as restorers decorated the interior in the appalling taste which you can see today, destroying in the process the original mosaics that decorated the archivolt and priceless frescoes of the fifteenth century which extended over every wall.

The history of the cathedral, and of its predecessors on the same site, is fairly well known and gives one an insight into the thousand-year struggle that preceded the triumph of Christianity. It is said that in the fourth century Constantine ordered the building of a small church at the extreme western end of the city, where the cathedral now stands, and thus at the greatest possible distance from the pagan temple of Venus, which is located at the bottom right-hand corner of our triangle. Tradition further has it that the Pope, Saint Liberius, conscious of the importance of combatting the old-established goddess, sent as a gift to the people of Erice an exquisitely beautiful statue of the Virgin for their devotions; on her forehead was engraved a star, whence came her title of Our Lady of the Star and the church's dedication to Our Lady of the Assumption. The image disappeared during disturbances in the twelfth century, and it appears that even during 800 years' sojourn it was unable to replace completely the memory of its rival at the other end of the city, for pilgrimages to the site of the Ashtaroth–Aphrodite–Venus continued up to and throughout the whole of the sixteenth century!

In the exterior of the south wall of the cathedral may be seen a row of nine curious marble crosses, another effort to draw worshippers away from the pagan goddess. A weathered plaque allows one to decipher that Constantine took them from the temple of Venus for the Virgin of the Assumption in the year 320; further on Pope John XIII, who ruled in the tenth century, apparently perpetuated their sacred virtue and the final date of the inscription is 1685. Although the crosses are still revered, especially on the Feast of the Assumption, the story of their origin is no longer considered credible, though no one has suggested an alternative.

From the cathedral it is easy to reach the left side of the triangle, a pleasant walk with occasional glimpses of courtyards on your right and a view over the restless treetops that clothe the mountainside on your left. Soon you reach the Porta Carmine, so-called from the adjacent church of that name originally built in the grounds of the Archbishop's residence. Now used as a school, one wall still retains the ancient string course and a *bifora* double window such as we saw in the belfry. A little further is Porta Spada, the Sword Gate, where the French were rounded up and butchered at the time of the Sicilian Vespers [*overleaf*]. Between the two gates the walk follows the line of the old walls, so old that in some of the sally ports the original Phoenician masons' marks, letters of the Punic alphabet, can still be

made out. At the Porta Spada the northern wall seems to be of Greek ashlar construction, while immediately round the corner one can step down to Phoenician courses built over a Cyclopean base. Useless to speculate who built these last; they appear in most European countries that border on the Mediterranean, in Sardinia, Minorca and the east coast of Spain. Samuel Butler, we hope with tongue in cheek, maintained that the Cyclopean walls of Erice were so called because the Cyclopes lived here, a simple enough solution.

Enter through the Porta Spada and the first two buildings on the left of the unspoiled country lane are churches. That of Sant' Antonio is deconsecrated, though the bells still hang in their place, and if you can get in you will be repaid with a view of fifteenth-century Byzantine frescoes and ceramic tiles of the following 200 years. Next door is Sant' Orsola [*opposite*] with its artfully neglected garden and a generally Oriental look, quite spurious but nevertheless attractive; inside are the images of scenes of the Passion, the celebrated *Misteri* that are carried in procession on Good Friday. Easter is indeed the time when ancient tradition may be observed in Erice; so, for example, the "gardens of Adonis" which are explained in another chapter are placed before the Holy Sepulchre at which the procession ends. The procession of the *Misteri* is so deeply rooted a part of Sicilian devotion that scholars have exercised their minds and imaginations for many years in tracing their source. The *Incontro* of the Virgin and her Son is fairly

24

confidently equated with the search of Demeter for her daughter; other theories compare the processions with the miracle plays of the early Middle Ages and Castelli sees in the riverside location of the celebration at Mazara the continuation of the spring festival of Anna Perenna, described by Ovid:

Idibus est Annae festum geniale Perennae,
Haud procul a ripis . . .

As you leave Sant' Orsola and begin to make your way down the right side of the triangle you are treated to one of the finest views that even Sicily can offer. In the foreground is the Quartiere Spagnolo, where a ruined barracks reminds you of the Spanish rule, yet another historic episode, and beyond it Mount Cofano rises sheer out of the Tyrrhenian sea, partly shielding the promontory of Saint Vitus. The rolling, cultivated plains that lead to Segesta are a patchwork of colour in springtime and the whitewashed houses of the tiny hamlets along the roadside look like strings of beads. Further on you come to the Church of Saint John the Baptist, with its mediaeval Norman portal on the east; it has little to interest the antiquarian, but one relic which will amuse the student of human failings. One of the sepulchral slabs in the interior, over the grave of a member of the Coppola family, has the date 1000 incised on it; only careful examination reveals that it was originally 1606 and that the alterations have been made with great skill; the attempt to add height, and therefore nobility to the family tree only shows that the later twigs would agree with Thackeray, that "it is impossible, in our condition of Society, not to be sometimes a Snob".

You are now about to reach the right-hand corner of the triangle, the site of the ancient temples to the goddess of love. The way lies through the charming municipal gardens of Balio, trees and rocks and winding walks on different levels, among busts of local worthies resembling the *hermae* of ancient Athens, with a few deficiencies in detail. The word *balio* is our "bailey" and in this case means the court of a feudal castle and there, at the eastern end of the park, rise the towers of a thirteenth-century castle, for long the residence of the governor.

What follows may be difficult to grasp, though I shall try to keep it simple. Every guide book I have read talks of the castle of Erice as though it was a single building, and all are agreed that it was built on the site of the ancient temple; thus we are told quite plainly that the castle of the *balio* occupies the site of the Temple of Venus. One can only conclude that some writers are given to copying from others or, more charitably, that they have invariably visited the city when the clouds were reducing visibility to a minimum. For the truth is that the Temple of Venus, and her predecessors, stood on an isolated pinnacle just off the tip of our triangle; it was on this pinnacle, over the ruins of the ancient temple, that a Norman castle was constructed, separated from the city by a ravine and drawbridge. Hence, when the Arab geographers Edrisi and Ibn Jubair visited this region in 1154 and 1184 respectively they described the castle and drawbridge; Ibn Jubair was enthralled with the beauty of the women of Erice—"may Allah make them slaves of the Faithful!"—and rather wistfully describes how they are sheltered in the castle at the first sign of danger and the drawbridge raised. The Norman castle and the castle of the *balio* are separated by about 200 yards and from the visitor's point of view are two distinct buildings, of different style and state of preservation. One is on the isolated pinnacle, the other on the mountain; one is partly ruined, the other well restored. The *balio* was built in the fourteenth century, by Frederick III and Martin of Aragón, when the twelfth century Norman castle was already abandoned. To say that the one was an outwork of the other may be true; but it is most discouraging to the tourist who consults his guide book, looks at two completely different castles, rubs his eyes and vainly consults his guide book again.

No view could exceed in grandeur that of the ruined Norman castle from the side of the *balio* [*Col. pl. IV(a)*]. At certain times the sheer rock is clothed with a primrose mantle, the blooms of thousands of wild fennel plants, the *marathon* that grows in Greece as well and must have carpeted the seaside plain where the Persians suffered their first defeat in Europe. The cultivated relation, *finocchio* in Italian, is a favourite addition to salads and soon palls on the foreign palate; the wild variety or *fella*, is inedible, but nothing is wasted in Sicily and its stems are said to make fine razor strops.

It seems as though there was a succession of temples to the goddess of love, all of fairly modest proportions; when Cicero was *quaestor* of

Lilybaeum, in 75 B.C., the temple was in a flourishing condition, but the economic depression and changes in maritime trade routes of the next generation led to the temple's decay and in A.D. 25 Rome was implored to do something about its threatened collapse from old age. This hardly accords with the pious fraud so earnestly preached by Christian authorities, both here and in other parts of Sicily, that the temple (or any other temple which still kept a reputation for miracles) fell down on the night of the Nativity.

Entering by a steep, right-angled stone stair, you come out into a great courtyard of ruins, decently clad in grass except where dense patches of red and purple and yellow wild flowers give the carpet its fortuitous pattern. Through gaps in the broken walls the panorama can be seen again, but inside there is no trace of the original temple. The site has been dug over at various times and finds are lodged in the civic museum and that of Trapani; all that remains here are a few Ionic column fragments from Roman times and the so-called Well of Venus, now believed to have been a granary, possibly the very one in which the tithes of corn were stored for the use of the priestesses. For the temple prostitutes could hardly have been expected to live on the offerings of wine which the customers carried up the hill,* nor on the daily sacrifice of two pigeons. The Elymians who, you remember, claimed to have come from Asia Minor, were the originators of temple prostitution at Erice, for the Carthaginians, who followed them and kept up the custom, practised it nowhere else. In Greece, too, it was found only in Corinth, where the original settlement, as well as the name, were distinctly pre-Greek.

Only the expert can tell, occasionally, where the various stones of walls and castle, including the part now used to house a wireless station, had their origin. There are certainly Cyclopean foundations visible here and there, but no one can possibly know the history of any stone that may have been used over and over again in the various reconstructions of the site. As you wander about you can reflect on the thousands of years through which the worship of Mother Nature, for she is the essence of all the goddesses that had their home here, persisted in this spot. From here her beneficent influence protected the sailors between Trapani and Carthage, Europe and Africa; Aphrodite Euploia, Goddess of the Fair Voyage, whose duties today have been assumed by the Madonna of Trapani, another version of Stella Maris. From this spot invisible lines connect you with the ports to which pious sailors carried the fame of the goddess: to Porto Venere near La Spezia, where her name is still preserved, and to Lerici a few miles away where the name of Erice, her home, has also survived. Her cult appeared at Cagliari in Sardinia and in many another Mediterranean harbour, and to

---

* Remains of thousands of clay wine jars, coming from as far afield as Rhodes, were discovered when the foundations of the Jolly Hotel were dug. Ericean antiquarians flippantly speculate on the potency of a man who has walked five miles and climbed 2,500 feet with a full wine jar on his shoulder.

this day she is commemorated in the name of Port Vendre, on the Franco-Spanish border, another Portus Veneris.

The cleft that once divided the pinnacle from the rest of Erice has been filled and there is no trace of the mediaeval bridge, nor naturally of the mythical one built by Daedalus. But it is instructive to remember how the Devil inherited the skills of the master craftsmen of long ago, and Devil's Bridges are common enough in southern Europe. It was thus but a short step from Daedalus to the Devil, and *Ponte di Dedalo* easily became *Ponte del Diavolo*, the latter name coming readily to the tongue of the Sicilian, whose favourite oath, in Samuel Butler's day, was "Holy Devil!"—*Santo Diavolo!*

To walk at random through the silent streets of Erice is an experience not readily forgotten. The distinctive pattern of the surface, white marble squares enclosing grey stone cobbles [*below*], blends so well with the mediaeval atmosphere that it is difficult to believe it was invented during the last century by a German engineer. Of the earlier Arab occupation there is little to see, at least outside the houses; within, the tapestry workers still reproduce oriental motives while *cous-cous* of rice and semolina is prepared in the earthenware Arabic *mafaradda*. Women's clothes, *ippùni, falàri* and *fustàna*, keep their original Arab names, while the country around is studded with villages, Rachanzili, Ralibbèsi, Rachàbbi, Racarrùmi, Ràbbatu, to name but a few, that also betray their Moslem origin. Place-names and words last longer than more tangible legacies, for they are not worth stealing; so the Byzantine rule of two centuries has left us only the names of a few villages, such as Sciannarini (Santa Irini) and Custonaci, and

of an occasional object, for example the paunchy vase called *rasta*, formerly *grasta* and originally *gastra*, which will be recognized by any gastronome.

Of all the doorways the most typical is the Spanish one with large voussoirs, often but imprecisely called Catalan, and occasionally wrought-iron window grills also serve to remind us of Spanish rule. One of its less pleasant aspects was the sale of a whole town by the sovereign in order to raise ready money; but so faithful to Aragón was Erice, that in 1407 King Alfonso decreed that it should forever be spared this humiliation. A Castilian king once said "Laws go the way that kings desire" and his remote descendant Charles V, Holy Roman Emperor, put Erice up for sale in 1555; the city ransomed itself and collected sufficient money to repeat the performance a hundred years later, when the Spanish viceroy sold it to Pandolfo Malagonelli of Florence. Reminders of Renaissance and Baroque builders are numerous, and the belfry of the Church of Saint Julian [*overleaf*] is one of the handsomest of the latter, as well as providing a landmark visible from many parts of the town.

A final review of Erice should be made at the Civic Museum and Library, where the genial Vincenzo Adragna gives willingly of his extensive knowledge. Though writers are apt to dismiss all but one of the exhibits, Antonello Gagini's Annunciation is by no means the only worthwhile piece. An Elymian double jar of the seventeenth century B.C. stands next to Phoenician amulets, Egyptian scarabs and fragments of amphorae with the Greek wine merchants' names still legible. On the wall there is a fragment of a Hebrew tombstone, reminding one that a Via Giudaica still marks the old Jewish quarter that lasted probably from Roman times until 1492, the date of the Spanish expulsion. Earnest—and imaginative—writers claim to distinguish a Jewish cast of countenance in the inhabitants of this street; I have been unable to confirm their observations. Other inscriptions are displayed, one written in a mixture of Latin, Greek and Hebrew and commemorating the Annunciation; the word "Jehovah" can easily be made out, as can the date and the year 5100 of the Creation, which fell somewhere in the twelfth century of our era.

Erice can well be described as potted history, but seldom has history been contained in such a charming pot. To leave it, even with the prospect of exploring more prodigious evidences of the past, is in some way like leaving one's fireside to admire the lights of Piccadilly Circus. Where else will you enjoy such quiet, breathe the fragrant scent of broom and pine, sharpened with the tang of the sea, look from Europe to Africa, or travel in an instant from twenty centuries before Christ to twenty centuries after? One leaves Erice with regret, as men have always done since the first Phoenician sailor waved to the great mountain, the last landmark of Sicily. Good-bye, Eryx! Good-bye, Ashtaroth! Good-bye, girls . . .

PART I—MAINLY PEOPLE

1 *The Greek and his Temples*

"Grammarian, rhetorician, geometer, painter, trainer, soothsayer, rope-dancer, physician, wizard—he knows everything. Bid the hungry Greekling go to Heaven! He'll go." To succeed in Rome, wrote Juvenal, you must be an Ionic Greek, combining Hellenic talent with Oriental superstition. The statement, true or false, gives me the opportunity of emphasizing a fundamental distinction in the Greek world, the rift between Doric and Ionic which affected language, architecture, ideals and settlement. The Ionians, regarding Athens as their parent city, colonized Asia Minor; the Doric Greeks, leaving their homes in the Peloponnese, migrated westward to Sicily and southern Italy. The origin of their mutual distrust goes far back into Greek history and has no place here; its culmination was staged in Sicily, where one of the world's decisive battles was fought.

Legends that featured gods and monsters were probably current long before the arrival of Greek colonists. Hephaistos, by some other name, busy at his forge below Etna, reflected in the red bellies of the clouds at night; his three helpers, the Cyclopes, against one of whom Odysseus won a battle of wits; the prehistoric cave dwellings along the Cava d'Ispica, south of Modica; all point to an indigenous population with its own folk-lore. But the Greeks were responsible for piquant detail: Hephaistos making his wondrous tripods, that fetch and carry of their own accord—"*automatoi*" the poet calls them; they have even been cited as the origin of the crest of Sicily, so like that of the Isle of Man [*below*].

In the eighth century B.C. the first Greek colonists came to Sicily from Euboea and settled at Naxos, the curved promontory that can be seen so clearly from Taormina. Later other coastal sites were appropriated, usually by Dorians, but sometimes by Ionians who may have left their original colonies in the Aegean to found granddaughter settlements in Sicily; the result was to bring Dorian and Ionian settlements into close contact and in this way the Greek proclivity for quarrelling with one's neighbours found a ready excuse. Did they come as an overflow from the tiny states of the home country, whose restricted acreage could no longer support a burgeoning population? It was not that they allowed the population to grow heedlessly: girls and other unwanted children were dutifully thrown out on the muck heaps, but busybodies would interfere with the practice of family planning. Or did they come as traders, in the wake of Cretans and Myceneans, who had established their trading posts many centuries before? Certainly the *Graeculus esuriens* had to live by trade, as we do today. Did not Aristophanes say "a man's fatherland is any place in which he is making money"? We need not take sides in this academic argument, but we may remember that the Vikings of another age were traders first and foremost, and colonists or pirates only from adversity.

Like the Phoenicians, who had begun to colonize the western end of Sicily about a century earlier, the Greeks chose promontories, off-shore islands or other easily defensible positions for their settlements; the sea was their life-line and even at the height of their power more than 90 per cent of them lived in coastal towns. The native population, Sikels who hardly feature in a historic narrative, were usually pushed into the interior, but intercourse with them, both mercantile and sexual, was usually maintained. It has been said that the Greeks had no salt in their native land, and certainly its large scale manufacture from sea water is possible only where there are flat coastlands, as in Sicily; it is true that the trade of salt boiler was known in ancient Greece, but the results of this industry must have been meagre and expensive. I cannot, however, see salt hunger prompting Greek colonization of Sicily any more than I would attribute the Roman conquest of England to a desire for Whitstable natives, or the Crusades to curry powder.

A number of misconceptions exist regarding the purpose and aspect of Greek temples, of which Sicily preserves so many examples. Few casual tourists are told, for instance, that the temple was not a place of worship; it was a home for the divinity, a strong-room for his or her possessions and an index of civic pride as much as piety. Access was strictly limited to priests, and the general public watched sacrifices at the nearby altar and joined in prayer outside the edifice, for Greek religion was essentially of the open air. Hestia, goddess of the hearth, was a very second-class deity and was not even mentioned by Homer.

Generations of travellers have described their reactions on seeing for the first time the tumbled ruins of Selinunte, the Vale of the Temples at Agrigento or the lonely grandeur of Segesta. Their psychic exhibitionism always includes their emotion on seeing "the tawny columns", "the honey-coloured stones" or "their warm, golden glow". Alas for our lessons in art appreciation! Those golden temples were built of a porous stone, whose crumbling is today made good by continuous restoration; in olden days it was protected by a layer of dead white stucco, on which triglyphs, antefixes, acroteria and even the famous metopes of marble bas-reliefs were emphasized with red, blue, yellow and black paint. Aesthetes recoil from faithful representations of the buildings they have been taught to revere, and even a coloured sketch can be relied on to curb an outbreak of *schwärmerei* in a group of German tourists. The same unpleasant truth must be told about their statues, which were also painted to make them more lifelike.

In one respect Greek building in Sicily stands supreme: everything is a little larger, a little grander, more ornate than in the home country. The prosperity of the western Greeks made them the *nouveaux riches* of the Hellenic world; even Euripides, in Shelley's translation, has the Cyclops say:

> *Wealth, my good fellow, is the wise man's God,*
> *All other things are a pretence and boast.*

but, as in other civilizations allegedly dedicated to the amassing of wealth, the quest for culture played an important part. Prominent men of science or art were invited for lecture tours and sometimes persuaded to stay, so that a westward "brain drain" had already begun. Aptly enough, Lampedusa called Sicily "this America of antiquity".

The size of some of their temples cannot but astound one at the engineering problems successfully overcome; Temple G at Selinunte, now lying with its six smaller companions in a vast desolation of building blocks, upset by an earthquake as though a giant's hand had tumbled a child's effort with one careless sweep, is seen to have consisted of elements of astonishing size and weight [*below*]. The appearance of destruction is enhanced by the partial

restoration of one of the temples. The drums which were superimposed to make columns, measure over ten feet in diameter and are anything from six to ten feet tall; their weight must therefore be around fifty tons. Compare this with the two-and-a-half-ton blocks of the Egyptian pyramids and you are faced with quite an engineering problem.

About five miles from Selinunte is a rock ridge that was used as a quarry until the day that the Carthaginians overran country and town, slaughtering and enslaving the inhabitants. In this quarry of Cusa you may still see upright drums partly chiselled out of the rock, and others abandoned on their way to the temple [*Col. pl. IV(b)*]; the first problem therefore is one of transport. There is no evidence of a metalled road from the Cusa quarry at Campobello di Mazara to Selinunte, so we must assume that the huge drums were trundled over the bare earth, which was possibly reinforced with pebbles; the fact that no abandoned drum is found lying flat is almost certain evidence that they were pulled along like a lawn roller, with or without a wooden frame as invented by Chersiphon in rebuilding the Artemision, better known today as the Temple of Diana of the Ephesians. We can only guess at the labour involved, the teams of oxen, or slaves for economy, the sleds and rollers that may have been used for the square or oblong blocks, and the years that were consumed in this unproductive effort. The raising of these monumental building blocks was probably less exacting; the pulley was known to the ancient Greeks and their wits were certainly sharp enough to realize that each added pulley doubled the lifting power, though it is not known, and indeed unimportant to know, whether they had incorporated several pulleys in a single block. Mortar was not used, and a wonderfully exact fit was obtained by rotating each drum on the one below until all irregularities had been ground away. Adjacent parts had slots chiselled for the reception of cramp-irons, secured with molten lead.

One of the consequences of this method of building was the systematic recovery of the cramps during the metal shortage of later years. The temple of Herakles at Agrigento is interesting in this respect, for many of the column drums have been chiselled out at their bases, presumably for this purpose. Von Pernull, however, obviously puzzled by the blunt conical ends of some of the drums, postulated that the Carthaginians had chipped away the bases of the columns in order to facilitate the pulling down of the temple. The hypothesis takes no account of the fact that this is the only temple at Agrigento that is damaged in this way, and that it is the last we should expect the Carthaginians to demolish, for Herakles was equated with their own god Melkart. A more likely explanation is that the iron and lead components were chiselled out in the sixteenth century, when the Spanish and Holy Roman Emperor, and Chief Vandal, Charles V was using the temple of Herakles as a quarry for his new harbour works at Porto Empedocle near by.

Components were assembled in a purposely rough state and then finished off before the stucco was applied. When you visit the wonderful temple of Segesta, solitary on its plateau, you will have the opportunity of examining a temple arrested in the course of construction. Note first that the columns are not yet fluted, for the longitudinal grooves could obviously be cut only after the drums had been fitted together, or, in the case of monolithic columns, after the capitals had been put in place. Next see how the abacus [*below left*], the square cushion above the capital and under the architrave, or stone beam, still has a stone roll at each angle, purposely left to avoid chipping a sharp corner during transport; before the building was completed the corners of the abacus would naturally be squared off. The stylobate, or platform, preserves the bosses that were left for lifting, to be levelled off when the building was complete [*below right*]; heavier blocks, to be seen for example in Agrigento [*below bottom*], had U-shaped grooves cut into

opposite sides and opinions are divided as to whether these are to accomodate lifting tongs or ropes. The problem was easy to solve: measuring the distance separating the arms of the "U" in several of the blocks pictured, I found differences of up to eight inches and no two blocks precisely the same. No tongs could be made to fit such a variety of slots, and ropes must therefore have been employed, a supposition strengthened by the way the inner margin of the "U" is undercut.

Fluting, or the cutting of longitudinal grooves in the columns, has given the experts another good excuse for a debate. It was originally claimed that stone and marble temples copied their primitive wooden prototypes so faithfully that the columns were made to represent hypothetical bundles of rods. When this claim was disproved a more reasonable suggestion was put forward: roof supports were assumed to have been squared in the early days, as mentioned in the *Odyssey*, and the four corners subsequently planed off to give eight sides though no one says why; a similar operation then produced sixteen sides and, to emphasize the pattern, grooves were cut in the flat surfaces. If you ask why all the columns you see in the remains of Greek temples have twenty, instead of sixteen grooves, I can only reply that the very earliest examples of Doric architecture did sometimes exhibit the sixteen sides. Twenty were chosen later so that the Greek desire for perfection could be satisfied; seen from the front or side, one groove lies in the exact centre of the column, while a diagonal view makes another groove appear continuous with the edge of the abacus. But a woman will give you a better explanation of the reason for fluting the columns, than any professor. Fat women favour longitudinal stripes on their clothing, thin ones prefer transverse. Doric columns, especially in the early days, were so stoutly made to support the weight of the superstructure that fluting was employed to give the illusion of grace, a far simpler device and no less credible than the many subtle optical illusions built into temples in comparatively early times.

Where the roof tiles of temples survive they repay a moment's attention. Measuring about two and a half by one and a half feet, they are made of baked clay, and those in the little museum of Selinunte show the origin of modern Roman tiling; the curved Arab tiling, commonly seen in Spain, seems to be derived from the Laconian, concave pattern; the flat ones are typically Sicilian, in that the "roofs" over the joins are shaped like a segment of piping. And, while in the museum, it is worth looking at some of the Doric patterns which were once friezes and antefixes and wondering how the colours have survived two and a half millennia.

Greek temples are majestic, even in their usual state of partial ruin; perhaps especially in that state, for the nearer to perfection, the sooner they pall. This heretical statement will shock the beginner and the expert alike; the *dilettante*, who has paid perhaps a dozen visits to Greece, Asia Minor and the western Greater Greece of antiquity, will probably agree that symmetric perfection, absence of variety and complete disjunction from the surroundings can become monotonous. Greek builders were not landscape gardeners; told to erect a temple on a plateau, in a valley, on a mountainside or on a hill-top, they would put up the same, or very nearly the same structure. Ruins, as Rose Macaulay was not the first to point out, have each their own charm, and Greek temples become less perfect and more seductive when they decay or become adapted to other uses by later generations. On a hillside at Agrigento stands the Norman Church of San Biagio [*below*], perfectly preserved, as are the foundations and *cella* walls of the Greek temple in which it was built. So charming has it become, standing near the ruins of one of the old town gates, that one feels no surprise at Captain Alexander Hardcastle's strange testament. With his brother, the Reverend Henry Robert, Alexander carried out one of the first programmes of scientific excavation, and in his will he wrote "Dear Agrigentine friends . . . bury me with a small window looking on to the ancient walls." His tomb is close by the Catholic cemetery, for naturally he could not be placed in consecrated ground, and in its northern wall a tiny window looks out on the Church of San Biagio, the rocky track scored with the wheel marks of the carts that brought the great stones from which its predecessor was built, the ruins of a city gate and the cleft that leads to the ancient sanctuary of Demeter. Only a man whose researches were inspired by love could demand, and deserve, such a tomb.

The continuity of Agrigento fills one with wonder. The sanctuary of Demeter preserves some Greek foundations amid the tangle of acanthus, geranium and a parti-coloured sweet pea, violet and purple, which the custodian planted and can no longer control. Behind, in the sea-shell studded Devonian rock face are prehistoric corridors with niches for the

crude statuettes of the Earth Mother and for oil lamps, whose soot still blackens the overhang. The so-called Temple of Concord, again, best preserved of all in Sicily, still has the arched entrances cut in the *cella* walls and owes its almost perfect state to its transformation into a Christian church in 597. According to the monk Leontius, the founder was Saint Gregory of Girgenti, who sought seclusion and turned his back on the slanders of the town, at that time under Byzantine domination. The Greek temples, ranged along the southern wall of the city, were then, as now, far removed from habitations and the inner face of the wall itself was used for Byzantine niche tombs that are still visible. Gregory chose the temple we now call, on insufficient grounds, "Concord" and exorcised the pagan demons, Eber and Raps, who were the occupants. Some believe that these demons were the successors of the Dioscuri, Castor and Pollux, for the church was dedicated to Saints Peter and Paul, who regularly took over from the Greek brothers. The matter would not be worth mentioning, were it not that the church came to be called Saint Gregory of the Turnips, from the story that the temple stood in a field of turnips at the time it was taken over for Christian worship. The story is a thin one; the ground is eminently unsuitable for cultivation, and a field that grew turnips one year would be likely to produce a different crop the next. Surely it is more reasonable to attribute the name *San Gregorio delle Rape* to the demon Raps, rather than to the Italian for "turnips"?

Another church, that of Santa Maria dei Greci, built into the only Greek temple in today's city on the hill, provides examples of almost every age. From the crypt a narrow passage leads, under the street, to the original stylobate and the bases of the columns of the peristyle, the upper parts of which are concealed in the Norman walls. On the south wall there is a Byzantine fresco and parts of a typical Saracen geometric pattern. The raised floor of the primitive *cella*, or inner chamber, has been cut away on three sides of what is now the sanctuary, possibly to make the customary half circle of seats for the deacons, and the beams of the wooden ceiling are painted in Romanesque style. The sacristy contains some of the cathedral treasures, spanning the centuries almost to the present day. The cathedral itself was so shaken by an earthquake that it is closed for repairs; its treasures are scattered among the Civic Museum, the new Archaeological Museum and Santa Maria dei Greci. A last item of news: dei Greci, "of the Greeks", has nothing to do with the temple that formed the original building, but is used because Greeks and Albanians fled to Sicily in the fifteenth century, when Turkish intolerance was making itself felt in the Balkans. The foreign communities were usually given a place of worship and to this day many of them preserve their own religion, language and costume.

2   Theatres—Fallacies and Phalluses

The first visit to a Greek theatre leaves one filled with admiration for the acoustics and the view, which are credited respectively to the builders' skill and sensibility. The former are certainly good, incredibly good in some instances; the latter is usually superb and quite unpremeditated, for there is no evidence that theatre sites were selected with this in mind. Theatres were built in a natural fold of the hillside, sometimes artificially prolonged to make the auditorium a little more than a semicircle; the earliest examples had no seating arrangements and the audience squatted on the steep hillside as best they could, for the theatre as we know it in its perfection came into being towards the end of the fourth century B.C. Now it is obvious that the fold of a hillside acts as a catchment for rain, and if the theatre is situated at the foot of the hill a minor storm may produce quite a cataract; the architect therefore had no choice but to locate his theatre as near the top of the fold as possible. From here the view was likely to be impressive; furthermore, as 95 per cent of Sicilian Greeks lived in coastal settlements, the nearest hillside fold was sure to face the sea, so that a breath-taking backdrop of light blue horizon, purple sea and curving coast line was superadded. At the outset, therefore, it would appear that the view from the auditorium was an unintentional by-product of the builder.

The argument gains support from the fact that the front seats were reserved for the most important civic dignitaries, as well as for distinguished guests, shown by the office titles still found carved on the seats of honour, or *proedria*, of the front row. From here, level with the *orchestra*, the dancing floor on which much of the action took place, a six-foot-high stage would obliterate the whole view. With a primitive, home-made astrolabe I was able to satisfy myself that the occupants of the first nine rows would enjoy no view at all, with a stage and scenery (*skene*) of only twelve feet in height. The occupants of the back rows, poorer citizens and possibly even women in the case of tragedies, were favoured with the glory of the land- and sea-scape, though I doubt whether they enjoyed it. For the beauties of nature are singularly neglected in Greek literature, though it debates the profoundest human and superhuman problems in masterly fashion. Here and there, as when Hermes, in the fifth book of the *Odyssey*, visits Calypso on her island, one reads a description of a charming, miniature dell; or rolling cornfields and fields of vines are described, but only in connection with the food and drink they will produce. The Greek theatre presented a religious festival, and the audience came to hear the plays, each presented only once during the great days of Greek drama, and not to gaze at the landscape.

To those whose ideas of Greek drama include the soulful actress and the stately chorus of robed elders, the truth will come as another shock. Women never appeared in the plays, female parts being taken by a male actor, who wore a distinguishing mask with resonant brass mouthpiece, for each personification. The chorus, all male of course, was an essential part of the play, and in the first tragedies only one additional actor, the "hypocrite" or answerer, appeared; the present meaning of the word obviously derives from the actor's habit of wearing a disguise. Later a second and then a third actor were added, each capable of changing his mask and being Agamemnon one minute and Clytaemnestra the next; the chief actor, however, was known by the corresponding Greek word "protagonist", which therefore has no meaning as the opposite of antagonist. Opinions differ as to whether the chorus were made up as horses or dressed as goats; certainly the word "tragedy" originally meant goat-song. The point is of no importance here, where only an attempt is being made to convey the flavour of the Greek theatre. Much of the action—and lack of it—took place to music, vocal with flute accompaniment, and the actor, as well as the chorus, could break into song when the excitement rose, though I doubt whether he would also dance with the handicaps of mask, towering wig, padding and *cothurni* or built-up boots that raised him above the chorus. As a schoolboy I used to welcome, as unnecessary to translate and therefore a free gift, such lines as

O tototoi popoi da Opollon Opollon

or simply

O popopopopopopopopoi.

Possibly a tune or a couple of dance steps would make them intelligible.

I have mentioned the religious nature of the play. Performances were given only two or three times a year, in festivals lasting several days, on each of which three tragedies, a satyr play and usually a comedy were presented. The satyr play, a pastoral tragi-comedy, was written by the author of the tragedies, so that *Cyclops*, from which I quoted earlier, would have followed on the tragedies by Euripides. In spite of the buffoonery which could accompany the antics of satyrs and Silenus, the theatre remained a sacred edifice for the duration of the festival and the audience was expected to behave accordingly, though free to applaud or condemn in an outspoken and even vociferous manner. And there seems to be no doubt that they not only enjoyed the superfluity of drama with which, squatting on the hillside or seated on hard benches, they were regaled, but absorbed enough to be able to discuss the drama intelligently and to appreciate comic allusions to a play that may have been presented once only, and that many years ago.

To many the emphasis on the organ of generation, signifying fertility and hence the god Dionysos in whose honour plays were performed, will seem strange, if not obscene. It should be a reminder that the Greeks who colonized Sicily were not the British who populate Belgravia, and that we must not peep at their customs through a veil of *pruderie anglaise.* A huge phallus was carried in the procession to the theatre, where a statue of Dionysos was placed in the orchestra so that he could have the best view of the performance. Let David Barrett describe some of the trappings of comedy:

"Traditionally, the comic actor wore tights over heavy padding . . . and a tight tunic cut very short so as to reveal an artificial phallus. The evidence is confusing, but it seems probable that this was still used as the basic costume in the time of Aristophanes, although it is clear that a character costume, which might include a long upper garment, was often worn as well. The phallus, the wearing of which was in full conformity with the ritual aspects of a Dionysian festival, could thus be concealed or displayed as appropriate. In *The Poet and the Women,* Mnesilochus comments pointedly on Agathon's lack of this masculine attribute. Subsequently he is himself dressed up in women's clothes, so that his own phallus is concealed until the famous disrobing scene. In *Peace,* the leading character, who flies up to heaven astride a dung-beetle, uses his phallus as a kind of joy-stick or tiller; and Procleon, in *The Wasps,* offers his to the flute girl as a hand-rope by which to pull herself up on to the stage. (Several episodes seem to imply that the phallus worn by comic actors was, or could be, a long floppy, flexible affair, and not a *phallus erectus*: this is to some extent confirmed by vase paintings.)"

The visitor must be careful to distinguish theatres which have been adapted by the Romans for their vulgar wild beast and gladiator shows; in these, the front rows have been cut away so that the nearest spectators should not become involuntary participants and

> *unwillingly represent*
> *a source of innocent merriment.*

Taormina, for instance, whose theatre was entirely rebuilt in Roman times and subsequently functioned as an Arab palace, has had at least eight of the front rows cut away and such a high *frons sceni* built that the famous view of Etna is obtainable only from the very back; the audience was therefore compelled to look at the arena, or what is now a gorgeous ruin. That, at least, is how you are supposed to view it; some say that it resembles a brickworks struck by lightning.

Of the genuine Greek theatres left in Sicily, the most charming and best preserved is the miniature gem at Palazzolo Acreide, about thirty miles inland from Syracuse. The diameter of the orchestra is only fifty feet, yet the auditorium is divided by staircases into no less than nine blocks, just like a grown-up theatre. The stage behind the orchestra still preserves a dozen cisterns of various depth, but no one has yet suggested their function. Adjoining the theatre and in surroundings which we can appreciate even if the Greeks could not, are mute witnesses of how they lived and died. A tiny open-air council chamber, or *bouleuterion*, adjoins the theatre and on the other side is the quarry, or *latomia*, again a toy copy of the great excavations at Syracuse. Votive niches and bas-reliefs can be seen as you enter the sheltered *latomia*, where the spring irises, lilac and apple blossom stand out among the wild flowers. Behind, you come upon the Greek necropolis, with its numerous entrances in the towering rock face. How aptly was it named, for it is indeed a city of the dead, with different districts, streets and alleys in its vast interior and groups of tombs, some with their stone slabs still in position, which are walled apart from the main throng and look out into the silent passages through stone screens.

Of other Greek remains, omitting the smaller objects that can be found in museums, there are enough to help in the task of reconstructing the days of the Greeks. At Morgantina, near Aidone—and you must remember to take either of two atrocious tracks to Serra Orlando on the *north* side of the Catania road—an important settlement has been excavated, centred round a forum either divided or entered by a monumental flight of steps, angled in two places [*below*] and 150 feet wide. Drains have been uncovered, not only the usual storm drains with stone slab covers, but domestic waste pipes, about ten inches in diameter, made of fitted clay sections, as still used in many parts of Sicily today, each provided with an oval inspection hole

and cover. Here and there querns lie about, of a type still used in country districts [*above*]; on either side are the slots in which handles are fitted when women or donkeys trudge round at the corn grinding. Wherever they are found in Sicily, querns are made of black lava, and from Greek times to the present day have had the grinding surfaces roughened with a claw hammer when they become too smooth. As the lava is apparently from Etna, one can visualize a flourishing trade in querns throughout the island; the peasants with whom I have spoken are unanimous that lava is unequalled as a grinding surface.

We have looked at some of the tangible legacies of Greece; what may we expect to find in the way of culture and custom? The millstones have their counterpart in the *amphorae* of ancient Greek shape, formerly shown to great advantage on the heads or shoulders of Sicilian damsels photographed by our parents, now, alas, replaced by plastic buckets of sickly hue. But field workers, who wish to keep their drinking water cool, bring it out in an *amphora*, often enough capped with a plastic cup. The *pithos* too, that great-bellied vat that you can still see at the palace of King Minos at Knossos, stands in the corner of many a farmyard, or stores grain in the cellar, identical with its remote ancestor, even to the collar of incised lines.

The people themselves often present features which we are accustomed to regard as classical Greek and their voices, according to an Italian guide book (*Consociazone turistica*), are sonorous, from the chest and full of diphthongs, reminding one of Greek mixed with the gutturals of throaty Arabic. The female voices usually have an elegiac cadency, even if back street brawls in Palermo sometimes result in stridency, with oriental dissonances. As we are completely ignorant of the sound of classical Greek, or the timbre of the voices of those days, we must not strain at the alleged similarity.

The worship of Adonis, at one time universal throughout the Near East and Grecian settlements, still survives in two forms in Sicily: "gardens of Adonis", small plots of vegetation intended to die through lack of soil, are still sown in spring as well as in summer, and various other customs mark Saint John's day, the 24th June. Now midsummer—Saint Jerome specifically mentions June—was the time for the rites of Tammuz or Adonis to be celebrated, and it has been suggested that Saint John was appointed by the Church to replace him, in the same way that Saints Peter and Paul were substituted for Castor and Pollux. Louise Caico went further and attributed the formula for corn division on Sicilian threshing floors to a similar classical origin: "In the name of God," they begin, and she equates this with the pagan "*Ab Jove principio*", though I should have thought the Arabic "*Bismillah*" to be a closer parallel and as likely a derivation. Another Sicilian ceremony, and a very moving one, is the *Incontro*; the Virgin is taken in procession through the town on Easter morning, looking for her Son, whom she eventually meets, to the great joy of the beholders. This is plainly the continuation of the classical tale of the search by Demeter for her abducted daughter Persephone; it is possible that the *Incontro* in that case formed the basis of the Eleusinian mysteries.

I have before me a recent newspaper cutting, whose headline reads "Girl breaks old Sicily custom: lover jailed". A wealthy young Sicilian had merely conformed with tradition, abducted the girl of his choice and then ... well, for the first time in history the bride refused to be made an honest woman; instead, the lover was charged with kidnapping and rape and is serving a sentence of eleven years. Now whatever acclaim may have greeted the sentence elsewhere in Italy, in Sicily strong feelings were aroused; imagine ours if the bowlers of a visiting test team consistently threw the ball and declared that straight arm bowling was out of date and uncivilized! But even this simile is a feeble one, for the Sicilian custom undoubtedly goes back to the ancient Greeks, and especially the Dorians. In Sparta, for example, the symbolic carrying away of the bride was genuinely enacted and the word for "marry", *harpazein*, literally meant, "to snatch away".

Until fairly recently Sicilian dead were carried round the village in an armchair, on their way to the cemetery; in Louise Caico's day, when the custom had already been forbidden by law, an exception was made in the case of the parish priest. From reliefs on Greek and Roman tombs it seems as though the custom, even to the escorting musicians, had descended directly from classical times. Hired mourners are another Sicilian speciality and can also be traced back to the ancient Greeks, among whom they were called *threnodoi*; apparently it is, and was, a genuine profession and not a method by which anyone could pick up a little pocket money.

Nelson-Hood, on whom Lord Nelson's dukedom of Bronte had devolved, described Sicily and the Sicilians as only a fellow-inhabitant could do. Dancing, he wrote in 1915, together with the art of cooking, has survived from Greek days as the chief of Sicilian accomplishments. Italian cooking is, to many foreigners, somewhat lacking in variety, and to those who seek stronger flavours and a more cunning use of herbs, the cuisine of Sicily, even in the best hotels, is a delightful experience. The wines, too, are of excellent quality and seem designed by nature to accompany the more robust offerings of the kitchen. Now however uninteresting ancient Greek cooking might seem to us, with its eternal barley and lentils, occasionally reinforced by dishes such as the Spartan black broth, consisting of pork, blood, salt and vinegar; however soon we would tire of the fish supplement and the cheese which then as now seemed to be a standard product admitting of no variety; it would appear that in those days too there were a few men with souls above the gossip of the market place and the politics of the city-state. For them Mithaecus wrote a book on the Sicilian cuisine and, according to Sladen, "a Sicilian cook in ancient Greece corresponded to a French chef today". Even Sicilian cheeses, the same author remarks, are varied today and were highly valued by the Athenians of classical times, possibly on this account. Their venerable story goes back to the *Odyssey*, for in Book IX, when Odysseus and his companions are trapped in the Cyclops' cave, the monster milks his ewes and goats, then "curdled the half of the white milk and, collecting it, placed it in braided baskets". The same baskets, pipes or pottles of plaited reeds containing cheese can today be bought in any country market and can be seen hanging in bunches from many a gate post. The curdling, so I understand, may still be performed with the sap of the wild fig tree instead of rennet, and here again we have a link

45

with the very earliest Greeks, for at the very end of the fifth book of the *Iliad*, we read how Paieon heals the wound inflicted by Diomedes on the war god Ares (who bellowed as loudly as nine or ten thousand warriors when he was hurt, and ran home to father Zeus), "and just as the sap * of the wild fig tree quickly curdles white milk, which is liquid but clots when stirred, so did he swiftly heal impetuous Ares".

Wild figs were, and still are, a prominent feature of the Sicilian landscape, and would have extended a homely welcome to the first Greek colonists. What other vegetation did they find? It is certain that the primitive cover had been considerably reduced by the Sikels and other early inhabitants, for valleys and hill slopes were so largely sown with corn that it was only natural for the newly arrived Greeks to take over the primitive goddess of fertility, and for Hybla substitute the corn goddess Demeter and her daughter Persephone. But in spite of the man-made clearings there were still wide stretches where cork tree and oak, chestnut and beech competed with the ubiquitous pine, while myrtle and wild olive, oleander, acanthus and asphodel clothed many an upland brae or river bank. Here and there the world of plants has been preserved on the silver coins which in Sicily reached a perfection never to be challenged before or after. The wild parsley which still grows in the valley of the Selinus, the river that gave its name to Selinous, now Selinunte, is faithfully reproduced in the abundant coins that are still being dug up among the ruins [*below*]; the date palm, probably introduced by the Arabs but possibly by the Carthaginians, figures on the

* Not the juice of the fig, as is often stated.

coins of the latter; and ears of corn are a frequent decoration on the coins of various settlements in this granary of the west.

It is difficult for today's traveller to picture Sicily as it greeted the earliest Greeks: take away the vast plantations of citrus that perfume great stretches of the countryside, the orderly rows of cultivated olive that were brought by the Greeks themselves and grafted with the wild variety for hardiness; the carobs, the great hedges of prickly pear and agave, which look so much at home though they are comparative *parvenus* from America; mulberry, date palm, cotton and sugar cane. Dismiss, too, the tidy vineyards, for the Greeks, if they did not bring the first vines, were certainly the first to use pruning in their viticulture. For all these substitute the primitive copses and forests and extend them over the eroded stretches too, and you will sense how man changed the face of a whole country centuries before the age of mechanization. It was, I suppose, inevitable in the days before man had seen the wisdom of replanting for posterity; for the needs of a million inhabitants, all requiring homes and fuel, and the navies which provided the greatest fleet of triremes afloat in the sixth century, speeded up the denudation begun by the Sikels, a process that was to gather impetus with each succeeding period of prosperity, except the Saracen. Not the least demanding in this long process were the requisitions of the greatest sea power of the sixteenth century and the Invincible Armada which lost the battle against its leaders' appalling organization and feeble tactics, and its enemies' brilliant seamanship.

3   *The Rise of Grecian Sicily*

Both the writer and the reader must be thankful that this is not a history book. The story of Greek Sicily, from colonists to catastrophe, is so involved that a mere perusal of dates and facts gives one no more idea of a 500-year adventure than does a description of the ductless glands of the divine enchantment of love. The skeleton of names, dates and facts is for examination candidates; decently clothed in a robe of anecdote and illustrated by the coins that survive from every age, dry bones may become the unobtrusive framework on which the imagination can build. For the whole of these 500 years east and west fought the first round of their long drawn out battle for the Mediterranean, and during the same period fought among each other with a ruthlessness and barbarity which rival the Carthaginian atrocities that have been so much more widely advertised. And as if this were insufficient expenditure of unproductive energy, each tiny state seethed with the effort of finding an answer to the question that has agitated the Greeks from Homer to the present day: which is the best form of government?

Somewhat to our surprise we find that the two forms which showed most vitality were the rule of a privileged upper class, and that of a dictator. Democracy, even the advanced variety of Athens, where as many as one out of twenty inhabitants had the franchise, seems to have come in a poor third. For about 200 years the plutocrats, known as the Gamori, controlled the destinies of Syracuse and of some later colonies. Horse breeders and keen sportsmen, the Gamori are immortalized by the chariot which appeared first on Syracusan, and later on many other coins. For they sent their teams, splendidly equipped and faultlessly trained, to compete in the Hellenic games and were so often victorious that they subsidized the best poets to compose odes of victory. On the reverse of a host of silver coins these chariots may be studied, some progressing at a walking pace, others in full gallop, down the straight or round the corners, where the *terma* stands upright, or lies in the dust, according to how closely the chariot has made the turn. All have one thing in common, the *Nike*, or winged victory with the winner's wreath, or sometimes a palm branch, floating above the horses and preparing to crown the driver. Occasionally, and much later than the period we are considering, *Nike* carries the *aphlaston* or broken off stern ornament of a warship as the sign of a naval victory; in my own collection she sometimes faces forwards, away from the driver, as though taking part in a triumphal procession [*below*]. In early Christian art we find the descendant of the selfsame theme, the martyr being escorted to Heaven by an angel, and receiving the palm branch or the crown of martyrdom from the same robed, winged figure.

The historic tyrants of Sicily make their entrance with Gelon, who, unsatisfied with ruling over Gela alone, took over Syracuse also. It was in the critical year 480 that the east made its supreme effort to crush the hungry Greeks who were everywhere nibbling at the territories of Persia and her satellites. With oriental attention to saving "face" after the débâcle of Marathon in 490, Xerxes King of Kings kept a special slave to tell him

daily: "*Despota mimneso ton Athenaion*—Lord, remember the Athenians." Some of us may remember him better as Ahasuerus, who numbered Esther among his wives; the Bible story tells us that he was uxorious and the history books hint that, with so many wives to be uxorious over, he lost his grasp of the reins of government. His navy was manned by Phoenicians, and while Xerxes advanced against Athens from the east his Carthaginian allies, themselves of Phoenician stock, invaded Sicily with an enormous host. Everyone knows of the battle of Salamis; Herodotus tells us that the equally decisive battle of Himera was won against the other claw of the pincers on the same day. Theron, tyrant of Akragas (Agrigento), hopelessly outnumbered by the host of the Carthaginian Hamilcar, was saved by the army of his son-in-law Gelon, who had arrived from Syracuse by forced marches. His swift and decisive action so impressed the Sicilians that his popularity was assured for ever, and his statue was the only one spared over a century later during one of Sicily's infrequent and short-lived interludes of democracy. To commemorate the victory Syracuse issued one of the world's best known and most beautiful coins, the "Demareteion" decadrachm. I should here explain the origin of the cumbersome terms by which these and similar coins are called. *Drachme* means a handful, and at some time in the seventh century it was decided that a certain weight of silver—about sixty-six grains at Athens—should represent the handful of iron spits which till then had been the unit of currency, and pretty awkward too. By prefacing the word with *di-, tetra-* or *deca-* two, four or ten drachm coins were denoted. And to this day, though probably not for much longer, British physicians and apothecaries measure solid quantities of drugs by the drachm, each composed of sixty grains.

The "Demareteion" was so named after Gelon's wife Demarate; having interceded with her husband to impose moderate terms on the vanquished Carthaginians, these presented her with a golden crown, from which were struck the commemorative coins. Being golden, it is more likely that the crown was exchanged for the appropriate weight of silver. It is unlikely that the beautiful head on the obverse was meant to represent Demarate herself and Quennell's hypothesis that her aquiline features argue Punic ancestry and hence solicitude for her defeated countrymen could hardly be maintained if a different model was actually used. This, at least, is the story told by Diodorus; other authors, such as Hesychius, state that the gold and silver were the offerings of personal jewellery made by Demarate and other ladies, in aid of the war effort.

Gelon was as able as he was unscrupulous, and laid the foundations of Syracusan prosperity by granting citizenship to the aristocrats of the other Sicilian Greek cities that he captured, much to their surprised gratification. Equally surprised were the common citizens, who had had no part in causing the conflict but nevertheless found themselves sold into slavery. It is easy to see what value Gelon placed on the proletariat as citizens in his

50

budding empire. His haughty spirit refused to bow to Sparta or Athens, to whom he promised a mighty reinforcement on condition that he was made supreme commander against the Persians; at the same time he was shrewd enough to prepare an indemnity in gold and an offer of submission to Persia in case the Greek allies were defeated. So far as we know, he was worsted only once, and that by his own wife. It is related that an intimate female friend told him what best friends are alleged to suppress, that he was afflicted by the appropriately Greek-sounding halitosis; returning home he reproached his wife with not telling him of this, whereupon Demarate sweetly answered that, from her inexperience of other members of the male sex, she thought all men must smell like that. A reply that must surely entitle her to the immortality of the decadrachm!

After Gelon came his brother Hieron, whose short reign is usually regarded as one of the golden periods of Syracuse. Obviously an amateur of the arts, he had the beauty of the Demareteia perpetuated in the tetradrachms struck soon after he came to power [*page 49*] and his court became the resort of leading Grecian poets; he was the first to tempt genius away from the mother country, in the same way as the United States once welcomed lecture tours by Europeans. Pindar began his career as a lyric poet before the Persian war of 480 and by the age of twenty-eight was celebrating Sicilian chariot victories and Sicilian flute players in his Pythian Odes. Soon after the war he went to Syracuse, where he produced Olympic Odes in honour of Theron's victory in the chariot-race and Hieron's in the horse-race. He remained closely connected with his patron, even sending him an ode as a sort of poetical letter. His interest for us probably lies in the demonstration of how athletic contests were linked with religion, and his belief, at a time when Athenian democracy was at its best, that the rule of aristocracy was preferable. Aeschylus, the first and most conservative of the great tragedians, was frankly modern by comparison, and Pindar could never have agreed with the criticism of the divine will implicit in the *Prometheus*. Both poets must have been at the court of Hieron at the same, or very nearly the same time, for both commemorated the founding by their patron of the new city of Aetna. We gather some idea of the brilliancy of the Sicilian courts from the fact that Aeschylus made the journey twice; the story that he left Athens because he was defeated by Sophocles and Simonides in the usual Athenian competitions, or because the wooden auditorium collapsed during the presentation of one of his plays, are unnecessary and untrue. He died at Gela from the strangest accident that ever befell a poet, and one who had survived the battles of Marathon, Salamis, Artemisium and Plataea at that. An unusually myopic eagle, looking for a rock on which to crack the tortoise it had picked up, mistakenly dropped its victim on the bald head of Aeschylus with fatal results, at least for the poet, and thus fulfilled the prophecy that he would die by a stroke from Heaven. The epitaph which he composed for his own tomb is illuminating in that it reveals the source of this aloof and irascible dramatist's real pride:

> One Aeschylus, Athenian born,
>   Son of Euphórión,
> Lies under this memorial stone
>   In Gela's fields of corn.
>
> At Marathon a sacred wood
>   His courage will declare,
> Or ask the Medes, with braided hair,
>   Who tried and found it good.*

After Hieron a spell of democracy set in and we hear nothing of tyrants for over half a century. Empedocles, the great philosopher of Akragas, was actually offered the tyranny after he had led the movement that expelled the oligarchy, but refused it, ever true to his principles. This is not the place to dilate on his achievements in the realms of philosophy, physics and biology, but many a teacher may take heart from his remark: "If I ever made someone think, I have justified my existence." He is said to have eradicated malaria from Selinous (Selinunte) by draining its marshes and to have ended his life by plunging into the crater of Etna, which threw up one of his brazen shoes. Both legends are doubtless untrue.

Sicily now provided both the excuse and the scene for the downfall of what Quennell has called the noblest of Greek democracies. This is not saying much, for a system under which the evidence of slaves is admissible in court only if extracted under torture hardly deserves the adjective, let alone the superlative. The Peloponnesian War, which the catastrophe at Syracuse rapidly brought to an end, was basically the final, fatal flare-up of Dorian and Ionian rivalry. Said the Spartan Brasidas to his men before the battle of Amphipolis, ". . . you are Dorians about to fight with Ionians, whom you are in the habit of beating", while the Athenian Thucydides makes Pericles taunt the Spartans for bringing allies to the attack while Athens usually defeats them on her own, even in their homeland. Pericles had been elected as head of state and, in Durant's words, "under him Athens, while enjoying all the privileges of democracy, acquired also the advantages of aristocracy and dictatorship". It was this democracy which, with the support of Alcibiades, made an unprovoked assault on the island of Melos whose Greek population, having surrendered at discretion, were killed if male and sold into slavery if female or juvenile. The same Alcibiades, aristocrat, idol of the people, leader of the gilded youth, dissolute spendthrift, general, traitor and double traitor, is made to say, again by Thucydides, "As for democracy, those of us with any sense at all knew what

* T. F. Higham's translation.

52

that meant ... but nothing new can be said of a system which is generally recognized as absurd."

Of course Thucydides made up speeches for his characters, but there is no reason to think that he did not reflect opinions prevalent at the time. The truth is that Athens, however benevolent her home rule might or might not be, was ruthless and grasping towards the rest of the Hellenic world, including her own allies. The glorious temples on the Acropolis were paid for out of the funds contributed by other states for mutual defence against Persia, as were wars of conquest undertaken against other Greek communities. Oblivious to the theme which her beloved dramatists so forcibly presented, that insolent pride carries the seeds of its own downfall, Athens pursued her imperialist ambitions.

4　The Downfall of Greece

Between Pericles and Alcibiades the government of Athens was in the hands of Cleon, first of a long line of demagogues and more imperialistic in outlook than any tyrant. Worse than most tyrants, he plundered the rich to gain the support of the poor, and he outdid the rest of the rabble rousers by being more eloquent, unscrupulous and corrupt. What Athens really needed was a Mark Twain. He wrote "All kings is mostly rapscallions", but he also wrote "Man is the only animal that blushes. Or needs to." In the fifth year of the war between Athens and Sparta, the former sent a fleet to fish in the muddy political waters of Sicily, where the Ionian men of Leontini (Lentini) [page 53] were at war with the Dorians of Syracuse. A stalemate ensued and at the Congress of Gela in 424 peace broke out and the Athenians sailed for home. The next attempt on Sicily, a typical imperialist adventure, was proposed by Alcibiades to an only too willing assembly. Syracuse was rich; Syracuse was a commercial rival; if Syracuse falls, the western Mediterranean is ours; corn, gold, slaves and soldiers can be obtained with little effort, and at the same time be denied to our enemies. Is it any wonder that Athens swallowed the bait, prepared an armada and, to quote Durant, "as if to ensure defeat, divided the command between Alcibiades and Nicias"? The ostensible excuse for the expedition was a quarrel between Selinous and Egesta (Segesta). The former had the support of Sparta, so Athens must naturally ally herself to Egesta; her ambassadors met the Egestan envoys at Drepanum (Trapani) and, for the social side of the meeting, a trip was arranged to nearby Eryx, where the treasures of Aphrodite's temple were displayed. It is not known whether the priestesses acted as hostesses on this occasion.

A mysterious epidemic of mutilation among the anthropoid herms that dotted the streets of Athens made the credulous citizens accuse their best general, Alcibiades, at the outset of the expedition. He deserted and left the army and navy in the hands of the irresolute Nicias.

Every guide book has an adequate account of the fate of the Athenians, to which we shall return in a later chapter. Some of the army might have been saved, but for Nicias' interpretation of an eclipse of the moon, which he thought was a warning to postpone his retreat. Plutarch, apparently just as credulous 500 years later, advances as an excuse that, at the time of the eclipse, Nicias did not have the services of a skilled diviner, his own having lately died. Thus it came about that superstition not only deprived the expedition of its best general but made sure that the next in command would surpass his own record of futility.

No sooner was Sicily saved from Athenian domination than Carthage saw an opportunity for wiping out the disgrace of Himera seventy-odd years before. Making use of the same perpetual quarrel between Egesta and Selinous, the Carthaginians came to the help of the former and utterly destroyed the latter. By 406 they had captured Gela and in the following year Akragas; from the accounts we have of pillage, fire and massacre in each city we may conclude that these barbarians were every bit as brutal as the Greeks. But they did not, as so often stated, pull down the temples, possibly because they were not worth the trouble of demolition; an earthquake in the fifteenth century completed their work. The Carthaginian invasion provided the opportunity for the restoration of tyranny in Syracuse and prepared the scene for its most colourful, if not most amiable ruler, Dionysus I.

> *...for I say that kings*
> *Kill, rob, break oaths, lay cities waste by fraud,*
> *And doing thus are happier than those*
> *Who live calm pious lives day after day.**

This was indeed a stage tyrant, a little larger than life, a little brighter than the footlights, an Iago with a sense of humour, a Macbeth, but less infirm of purpose. He came to power by accusing the generals of Syracuse of incompetence in the face of the Carthaginian menace, was granted a bodyguard, established himself in power, was beaten by the Carthaginians and bought them off at the expense of the other Greek states. He distributed others' property with the same generosity and peopled the cities he had gained with citizens and slaves from elsewhere. Aiming at the expulsion of the Carthaginians, he first secured Syracuse with walls of prodigious length and a castle of enormous strength, then advanced to the attack. I have told how he captured Motya; he was less successful against Lilybaeum (Marsala), where Carthaginian reinforcements drove him out and followed him across the length of Sicily, to besiege him in Syracuse. There he was saved by his new walls, aid from Sparta and plague among the besiegers. His ambitions were not confined to Sicily and he extended his empire to the mainland; besieging Rhegium (Reggio di Calabria) he offered freedom to the inhabitants in exchange for their treasure and then, in possession of the ransom, sold them as slaves. Many who have not been accused of despotic behaviour have acted identically, for example Ferdinand the Catholic at the capture of Málaga. In order to carry out his scheme of expansion, Dionysus became the first Sicilian to engage Samnite and Italiot mercenaries but, as has usually happened, found others of the same race employed by the

* Euripides: *Bellerophon*. Trans. J. A. Symonds.

55

Carthaginians. This fact gave rise to a curious coin, not too rare from the collector's point of view. We have seen how the Carthaginians coined a tetradrachm, with horse and palm tree on the reverse and a copy of the Syracusan Arethusa, dolphins and all, on the obverse [*pages 18 and 19*]; while they remained Carthaginians the mercenaries were paid in this war currency, and when they changed sides demanded payment in the same coin. So Dionysus had to have Carthaginian coins specially minted, leaving out the "*Ommachanat*", in order to pay his troops with coins of which the obverse was the copy of a copy of a Syracusan tetradrachm! A parallel can be found in more recent years, for Ethiopians still prefer, and in my own experience used to insist on being paid in Maria Theresa *thalers*, coins first struck two centuries ago, and still being minted exclusively for the Abyssinian market.

He professed interest in Plato's views on government and invited him to Syracuse; he probably regarded himself as an embodiment of rule by the fittest to govern and no doubt agreed with the philosopher that men are created unequal. Their quarrel may have been based on personalities, not principles, though it was reported to have been precipitated by Plato's criticism of dictatorship. "Your words," said Dionysus, "are those of an old dotard." "Your language," said Plato, "is that of a tyrant." * The unfortunate philosopher was thereupon sold into slavery by his host, who was never averse from turning an honest penny; luckily he was ransomed by a Cyrenean—another carried the Saviour's cross 400 years later—and returned to Athens to found the namesake of all academies.

Staying at the court of Dionysus was a risky undertaking and one hopes the occasional rewards were worth while. There is a quarry in Syracuse named *Latomia del filosofo*; the eponym is said to be, not "philosopher" but Philoxenos, a well-known poet of Cythera. He was bold enough to criticize a poem of his patron's and was summarily sent to work in the quarries; some time after, Dionysus relented and summoned him back to court, made much of him and asked him to comment on another of his efforts. Philoxenos got up, shrugged and "Back to the quarry, boys" was all he said. The tale at least reminds us of the tyrant's literary ambitions, the cause of much amusement in Greece and eventually of his death; his tragedy, *The Ransoming of Hector*, was awarded first prize at an Athenian festival, allegedly for political reasons, and Dionysus celebrated his success so enthusiastically that he contracted a fatal fever. It was his playful habit to test the courage and constancy of those around him. On one occasion he asked Aristides the Locrian, one of Plato's companions, for the hand of a daughter in marriage. "I had rather see the virgin in her grave than in the palace of a tyrant," replied the rash visitor. Dionysus thereupon had the sons of Aristides put to death, afterwards repeating the request; he received another refusal and history is silent about his next move. The well known

* Durant, after Diogenes Laertius. Plato was probably forty-two years old at the time.

story of Damon and Pythias (more properly Phintias) was also enacted at the court of Dionysus: Phintias, having been condemned to death for conspiracy, asked for a day's leave of absence in order to arrange his affairs, Damon offering himself as a hostage for his friend's return; Phintias returned and Dionysus, in Durant's words, "as surprised as Napoleon at any sincere friendship, pardoned Phintias, and begged to be admitted into so steadfast a comradeship".

There cannot have been many dull moments at the tyrant's court, even for those who were in favour. One of his courtiers, having expressed sycophantic envy of his happiness and good fortune, was royally entertained at a banquet. His complacency was, however, disturbed by Dionysus drawing his attention to the sword which hung above him, suspended by a single hair. Need I add that the courtier's name was Damocles? In similar, humorous vein he stripped the golden cloak from the great statue of Zeus, saying that it was too cold in winter and too warm in summer and substituting for it a woollen one, which would serve the whole year round. Consciously or unconsciously, Henry VIII plagiarized, when he seized the golden shrine of the Venerable Bede, remarking that it would be of more use to him than to Bede. Like all but the most benevolent tyrants, including Louis XI, Dionysus became increasingly suspicious: Cicero relates that he had a prison constructed in such a way that the slightest whisper would be carried to a small room in which Dionysus was accustomed to sit; the tale has been adapted to the great vent in one of the quarries. Leaving aside the murder of his mother-in-law, which might seem vaguely humorous to those who have the patience to study his family life, I shall end my account of this remarkable man with an anecdote that is so blatantly fabulous that one wonders how much else is true: as he became increasingly suspicious he allowed only his daughters to shave him and to be doubly safe made them use red-hot nutshells instead of a razor.

Subsequent rulers of Syracuse, good or bad, benevolent or tyrannical, are necessarily an anticlimax. We could no doubt find much of interest in the lives of Dionysus II and Dion, of whom Plutarch has much to relate. We should note the arrival of Timoleon from Corinth in 344 B.C. and the rapidity with which he expelled almost every tyrant in Sicily; becoming blind, he was still brought to the great theatre of Syracuse to listen to the debates and guide the policy of the democracy which he founded and which lasted at least twenty years. The slots in which the bearers rested his litter are still shown to the credulous.

One of Plutarch's tales relates to Timoleon's original advance on Syracuse from what is now Taormina. Choosing the route round the western side of Etna, he encountered and defeated the enemy near Adranum (Adrano), whose inhabitants received him with enthusiasm. They told him of the favourable portent which had been observed, that the doors of their temple flew open of their own accord, that the javelin also, which the god held in his hand, was observed to tremble at the point, and that drops of sweat had been seen running down the face. Is it coincidence that Louise Caico, living less than fifty miles from Adrano in the year 1910, tells of the local patron Saint Calogero, that "he has a black face, and iron head and perspires when he does a miracle"? Later she adds that the handkerchiefs with which the sweat was "mopped off the iron face" were highly prized.

After the brief democracy established by Timoleon, power fell into the hands of the able but ruthless Agathocles. One is intrigued by the fact that his third wife, Theoxena, was an Egyptian princess, daughter of Ptolemy I, and some say that, being homesick, she introduced the papyrus plant into Sicily, where it once flourished widely and may still be seen near Syracuse; the more usual explanation, of course, is that it was brought over by the Arabs in order to make writing material. Agathocles was the first to incorporate the Trinacria emblem in his coinage [*page 32*], whence it was later copied by Julius Caesar and thence by Marabitti; the last-named, a Sicilian sculptor of the eighteenth century, was commissioned to produce a Sicilian coat of arms by Maria Carolina, Queen of Naples and sister of the ill-fated Marie Antoinette.

The last great tyrant of Syracuse was Hieron II, who ruled both wisely and well for fifty years; because of this he is poor material for the biographer. He is memorable for three reasons: his alliance with Rome during the first Punic War; his concern for the capital city, resulting in a show-place that has seldom been equalled; and his patronage of the arts and sciences. Representative of the former is Theocritus, the greatest of Greek pastoral poets, who was born in Syracuse and wrote his first poems, including one which mentions Hieron, in Sicily. King Hieron is said to have been related to Archimedes; at all events his benign rule provided the stability wherein the greatest of the scientists of antiquity could work. One would like to tell more of the king, but little has come down to us; newspapers of today are not the first to discover that immorality is the readiest passport to immortality. Hieron's virtue seems to have included even his home life, thus possibly establishing a precedent among Hellenic rulers; he was modest in his wants, frugal in his habits and probably devoted to his wife, whose name still adorns her front-row seat at the theatre and the tetradrachm which bears her portrait, in the Hellenistic style, on the obverse [*opposite*]. The usual chariot on the reverse has dispensed with the winged victory, but instead carries the words "*Basilissas Philistidis*", a rare honour for, so far as I know, only Agathocles was thus glorified, before Philistis.

Archimedes was by far the more colourful character. We all learned at school how his engines baffled the Roman besiegers of Syracuse time after time, and how he was killed by an impatient Roman soldier whom he had told not to walk on the diagrams he was drawing in the dust. His contributions to civilization did not, however, comprise only methods of annihilating one's enemies or of protecting oneself. His improvements on the fortifica-

tions of Syracuse, and especially the castle of Euryalus, are indeed remarkable; but the discerning student attaches far more importance to his less
practical achievements, especially his original work in pure mathematics.
Archimedes was of the same mind, for he declared that "every kind of art
which was connected with daily needs was ignoble and vulgar"; such con-
tempt of utilitarian science accords ill with the story of his joy at the
discovery of the principle of specific gravity. Hieron had ordered a golden
crown, or possibly one of electrum, an alloy of gold and silver; when the
finished article was delivered, the tyrant had his doubts as to whether the full
quantity of gold had been used and suspected that the jeweller had used
more than the specified quantity of silver, retaining the surplus gold. The
problem was handed to Archimedes, and the solution is said to have
occurred to him in his bath: as he immersed himself he noted that the water
rose by a certain amount; from this he argued that a certain bulk must
displace its own volume of water; a crown made of silver will displace as
much water as the same crown made of gold, though the weights would of
course be different. By experimenting with different proportions of silver
and gold Archimedes was able to prove that Hieron's crown had been made
with an unduly high proportion of silver, naturally to the craftsman's advantage. The story has it that Archimedes, once the idea had occurred to him,
leapt out of his bath and ran home naked, crying *"Eureka, Eureka*—I have
found it, I have found it." It is an unlikely tale, for he was far prouder of the
theorem which follows. Perhaps his ready wit invented it to explain to an
inquisitive wife why he was coming home without his clothes; other reasons
were doubtless possible.

His greatest achievement, in his own eyes, was the proof that both the
area and volume of a sphere inscribed in a cylinder were in the relation of
2:3. Today we regard it as fairly elementary, but we must remember that
our notation, algebraic symbolism and conventions regarding the position

of numerator, denominator and powers of a number were unknown. This is how we should go about it:

The height of the cylinder (h) equals the diameter of the sphere, i.e. twice the radius (r).

The volume of a cylinder is $\pi r^2 h$, or $\pi r^2 \times 2r$, or $2\pi r^3$, and can be expressed as $\frac{6}{3}\pi r^3$.

The volume of a sphere is $\frac{4}{3}\pi r^3$.

Therefore, discarding $\frac{\pi r^3}{3}$ which occurs in both formulae, the ratio of cylinder to sphere is as 6:4, or 3:2.

Archimedes had a far more difficult task, though we may think that his book on Spirals and his anticipation of the infinitesimal calculus show greater brilliancy. In any case he asked that the sphere in the cylinder should be placed over his grave. He was not to know how he would die, but he would have been happy to know that the Roman commander Marcellus carried out his wish while deploring the unnecessary death of a genius. Over a century later Cicero discovered this geometrical tombstone overgrown with brambles; today a square in Syracuse and the indebtedness of mankind are his only memorials.

Among Greek survivals in Sicily are the *Incontro* of the Virgin and Son, so closely modelled on Demeter's quest for Persephone; an archaic statue of Demeter holding the infant Persephone, formerly doing duty for Madonna and Child in the Cathedral of Enna; and the resemblances, often quoted, between the festivals of Isis and of St. Agatha, patroness of Catania. Aphrodite and her sacred myrtle have survived as the Madonna delle Mortelle at Villafranca; and the death-fires, of which Nelson-Hood was told, go back to the *ignis fatuus* of the Romans and the Greek *pyrsoi*.

5   *In the Roman Orbit*

To the foreigner it is obvious that Sicily is a part of Italy; so obvious, in fact, that he never gives the fact a moment's thought. In the same way, a foreigner at the close of last century would have regarded Ireland as a part of Great Britain. The parallel between Ireland in the nineteenth century and Sicily after the Punic Wars is indeed a close one: both had their own language; in both a class of foreign landowners flourished while the peasantry remained poor or became poorer; and both were divided into areas of varying attachment to the conquerors. Of course there were differences: no historic analogy is more than superficial, as we can readily deduce from Plutarch's comparisons of the various subjects of his biographies. It may be urged that England's rule in Ireland was milder than that of Rome in Sicily but, taking the difference in epochs into consideration, this is not necessarily so.

A ready-made excuse for the trial of Roman against Carthaginian strength was provided in Sicily: some Campanian mercenaries, who described themselves as Mamertines, Sons of Mamers or Mars, had occupied Messina and neighbouring areas and were making a nuisance of themselves. Having provoked almost everyone else in Sicily they found it expedient to employ a protective Carthaginian force; more easily hired than fired, the Carthaginians refused to leave when requested, and the Mamertines appealed to Rome. The result was the first step towards Roman domination of the western, and part of the eastern world, with immeasurable consequences in language, law and literature for the following twenty-two centuries. Roman rule in Sicily, contrary to what is automatically repeated in so many books, was on the whole a benign one, and appears to have been welcomed in a country that had been torn by Greco-Carthaginian wars for over a century.

It is to Plutarch that we have to turn for a Greek's impression of events that had taken place 300 years earlier, gleaned no doubt from the history books of the first century of our era. His biography of Marcellus is so relevant to Sicily that it may suitably open our survey of six centuries of Roman rule. In the first Punic War Rome had driven the Carthaginians from Sicily; in the second the Carthaginians, under Hannibal, carried the war to Italy itself, where Marcellus fought with distinction in a series of defeats. The effect of Hannibal's victories was profound; Rome's friend, Hieron II, was dead and his successors at Syracuse, with astonishing lack of common sense, now showed themselves favourable to Carthage's renewed ambition. At this stage Marcellus was dispatched with an expeditionary force to ensure that Sicily remained faithful to her Roman alliance. We cannot but admire, in passing, the courage and wisdom of Rome's strategy, in sending expeditionary forces to Spain and Sicily at a time when the formidable Hannibal was ravaging the home country.

Marcellus was a gentleman, in an age when only language distinguished the civilized from the barbarian. He wept when Syracuse fell to his troops, at the thought of the inevitable suffering and destruction; above all he wanted to spare Archimedes, whose genius had defeated Roman siegecraft for so long. "*Noli tangere circulos meos,*" the old mathematician is reputed to have said to the soldier who killed him, considerately using Latin that is intelligible to the fifth form. I have mentioned that Marcellus himself saw to it that Archimedes' grave was adorned with the emblem he had selected; he also ensured that the sack of Syracuse was incomplete, so that the city's reputation as an artistic centre was uninterrupted. Hence the Emperor Augustus, in Rome two centuries later, would retire to an apartment at the top of his palace which he called his "Syracuse", or art gallery, when he wanted to be alone.

Under Roman rule slavery was an integral feature of the economy, as indeed it was in every other contemporary state. The Slave Revolts of Sicily, though suppressed with some difficulty, may have been partly responsible for a more enlightened treatment of the unfortunates. The first, and more famous, was that of Eunus, whose statue stands as a memorial to the Sicilian's striving for independence, in the shadow of the castle of Enna. A prophet and a juggler, he had the good sense to leave the fighting to a Cilician called Cleon and matters of policy to Achaeus, a Greek slave; as he himself was a Syrian he can only be regarded as a proxy prototype of the Sicilian freedom fighter. A sign of cheap slave labour was the system of *latifundia*, still surviving today as *latifondi*, in which vast areas were so profitably farmed under individual owners that the small landholder was frozen out. The system persists today in a modified form and rouses the wrath of literary liberals, whom the Sicilians themselves call "the Via Veneto communists". I doubt though whether it is quite as soulless as it was in Roman times, when the estate property, or *instrumentum*, was classified as *vocale* (slaves), *semivocale* (cattle) and *mutum* (tools and furnishings).

I have said that Sicily obtained considerate treatment on the whole; exceptions were bound to occur, and the case of Verres is so well documented that writers are apt to regard it as typical. Supreme power, always with the possibility of appeal to Rome, was vested in the *praetor*, under whom a *quaestor* supervised each half of the island. There is no doubt that Verres was a scoundrel, and if we are to believe Cicero, he used the office of praetor to rob, torture and kill both Sicilians and Romans, to seduce wives, daughters and sons indiscriminately, and to divert money allocated to the defence force into his own pocket, assuming that he had pockets and did not entrust a slave with his coins, or keep his small change in his mouth, as did the Athenians at one time. The episode of the starved and undermanned navy provides a human touch, for the sailors who put in at Pachynus (Pachino) were so hungry that they ate the roots of a wild palm which grew, and still grows, along the southern coast of Sicily. Of the thousand species, this particular tree figured on the coins of Camarina, a mere thirty miles

away, in the fifth century B.C. Another indictment at the trial underlines the Roman aspect of dignity that they called *gravitas*: Verres, says Cicero, actually appeared on the seashore in sandals, a long Greek tunic and a purple cloak, leaning on a woman. The last item was apparently not the worst, or at least would not count so strongly, for again he thunders "You, a praetor, showed yourself in your province in a tunic and purple cloak". Reading Cicero's orations you would imagine that wearing Greek dress was as reprehensible as having a Roman citizen crucified, a punishment reserved for slaves and foreigners.

Our next landmark is Hadrian's visit of A.D. 126, on his way back to Rome from Greece and the Near East. The most widely travelled of the Roman Emperors, he supervised the administration of every region in person, advertising his policy by special issues of coins, one of which is shown. The obverse shows the head of this, the first bearded Roman

Emperor and the reverse bears the inscription COS III, thus emphasizing the polite fiction that he was a constitutionally elected consul in his third term of office. The beard was quite a momentous growth, for it had become unfashionable since Alexander the Great ordered his troops to be clean shaven, to prevent an enemy obtaining an unfair advantage in seizing a soldier by the beard. Hadrian went so far as to make it obligatory wear for officers, and in consequence the beard became fashionable under his and subsequent reigns. We may be sure that he visited Sicily as he did every other part of the empire, with a view to having it run on businesslike lines; the country probably benefited greatly from his enthusiasm for Greece and its civilization, especially as Greek was an official language, along with Latin. Combining a streak of mysticism with his practical and literary gifts, we find him climbing Mount Etna so that he could view the dawn from a height of 11,000 feet.

The Roman contribution to art in Sicily was small, which is not surprising in view of the Greek superiority in that field. In engineering, however, they left their record here as everywhere; the amphitheatre, devoted to wild beast and gladiatorial shows, is a typical Roman product and was often erected alongside a pre-existing Greek theatre. Ruined remains are visible at Catania and Termini Imerese, but the only one worth seeing is that of

Syracuse. Greek theatres, as mentioned earlier, were sometimes altered to accommodate the same spectacles. Aqueducts are still visible here and there, notably at Taormina, and Roman roads formed the first overland links between important centres; the existing one from Messina to Palermo is largely built on the Roman foundations of the Via Valeria and in the ruins of Tyndaris (Tindari), which overlook the sea on the right, are the well preserved remains of a Roman basilica [*below left*] and several houses. One of them, presumably the property of a wealthy man, has its private bath wing where the ravages of time display how hot air circulated under the floor and in the walls of the *calidarium* [*below*]. Two Roman tombs still stand in Agrigento; their occupants are unknown, but civic self-glorification has named them the Tomb of Theron and the Oratory of Phalaris. The latter is particularly interesting, as the Roman body of the tomb is incongruously crowned by a groined, mediaeval Gothic roof. Perhaps the most ingenious and possibly least appreciated Roman invention is shown [*overleaf*]. Main roads in Roman cities inevitably became deeply rutted by heavy carts, and in wet weather resembled rivers with a few stepping stones that must have presented quite a problem to chariots with comparatively low axles. Visitors to Pompeii, in fact, often express astonishment that horse-drawn vehicles could negotiate the main streets. At Solunto, pedestrians on the side streets

who wished to cross the main road did so over a removable bridge that fitted by means of prongs into the permanent sockets [*above*] at street intersections, a primitive precursor of London's Tower Bridge.

The story of the royal hunting lodge near Piazza Armerina is a thrilling one, and perhaps the most exciting episode concerns the identity of the owner and its revelation. In a wooded valley at the foot of Mount Magone there stood a modest building of the second century A.D., and in the third a huge and sumptuous villa was built over it by the Emperor Maximianus Herculius, who shared the rule of the Roman empire with Diocletian. The site was only three miles from the ancient town of Philosophiana, now Soffiana, which is recorded in the itinerary of Antoninus Pius in the second century. The villa, which was a hunting lodge used only between August and October, was inhabited until the Arab invasion of the ninth century and came to be known as the *palatium*, for obvious reasons; it seems to have been last mentioned in a letter of Saint Gregory the Great, whose mother was a Sicilian heiress, living in the sixth century. This was the Pope, famous in our history books, who saw the fair-haired slave children on sale in the Roman market, remarked "*Non Angli sed angeli*" and sent Augustine to England to convert the heathen. Another link with Sicily. The abandoned buildings were populated again under the Normans, when incidentally considerable damage was done, and a whole town grew up in the ruins of this single *palatium*, from which it took the name Plàtia. Another destruction, this time by William the Bad, in order to teach his obstreperous Lombard followers a lesson, resulted in the colony being moved to a new site, the present Piazza Armerina. It is possible that the word Piazza is in this instance derived from Plàtia, or even from Pluzia, one of its more ancient

66

names acquired from its reputed opulence (Greek *ploutos*, wealthy); anyone who has climbed to the cathedral will scarcely credit the normal meaning of Piazza as a broad, open space.

Hardly had the settlement been moved—and this explains why today's inhabitants of Piazza Armerina still speak a dialect nearest to the Lombard and Piedmontese and why they are so frequently blond and burly—when squatters began to live in miserable huts in the villa. Then a great landslide buried hovels and palace alike and all memory of the latter was lost until sporadic excavations were prompted by the persistent uncovering of portions of the ruin in the eighteenth century. The landslide tells us much about the history of Sicily, whose mountain slopes were denuded for centuries in order to build triremes, houses and outbuildings, to provide fuel and even for export, while no one thought it worth while to plant a tree, except possibly the Arabs. For the *Hadith*, or reputed sayings of Mohamed, contain the following: "He who plants and cultivates a tree shall be rewarded, just as he who prays at night and fasts by day and he who spends his whole life in war on the paths of the Lord."

It is only recently that the imperial villa has had its treasures brought to light and adequately protected from the weather, while raised walks have been provided to allow the visitor to look down on the surviving mosaics. Splendid as it is today, its original appearance, with marble walls and ceiling mosaics as well, must have been sumptuous indeed. In the rush of the standard tour of Sicily the visit to this relic of the great days of Rome is unique. The quietness, the shade of oak and pine and cypress, the view southward over the miniature, fertile valley, the splash of water and the song of birds will persuade you that the site was chosen for reasons other than hunting only. The bird song is an especially welcome change from the rest of the island, where the smaller species are extremely rare, inevitable in a poor country where the joyful notes of the lark or nightingale serve to attract the protein-hungry hunter. They say that sparrows are not found in Sicily, and I was therefore all the more pleased to find a pair enjoying their traditional meal in the road, not two miles from Cape Passaro; as *passero* is Italian for sparrow, it made me wonder whether the headland should not have its spelling seen to.

Were I a unit in a conducted tour, I should fall behind the party long before it reached the villa along the woodland path, and spend half my time wandering round the ruins and only half in studying the mosaics. Outside, one may identify the two aqueducts that were needed for the enormous staff which surrounded a Roman emperor, even on holiday; the bathing wing with its array of flues, like organ pipes, visible in the broken walls;* the monumental entrance and the two companionable latrines, the larger a twelve-seater, with water-borne sewage laid on. Tracing the water supply by

---

* These are liable to be confused with the rows of clay pipes used inside vaults and domes in order to lighten the structure, an early form of tubular construction.

67

means of the original lead pipes (a sure sign that the villa was buried and forgotten in Renaissance times, when lead was at a premium) leads you to the fountains which played in various parts of this hunting lodge—in one part, the court called *xystus*, as a background to dancers. One of the most important features of this vast complex, which should not be overlooked in ·the excitement of seeing the mosaics, is the great *triclinium*, with its three semicircular apses arranged in clover-leaf pattern, opening off the *xystus*. We shall see the same plan again and follow some of the steps by which a Roman dining room evolved into the world's largest church, the basilica of Saint Peter, in Rome.

How can I convey the wonder of the mosaics? [*Col. pl. V(b)*] Even the best reproductions, and some of them are very good indeed, cannot inspire the same emotions as the bird's-eye view of room after room, or the long passages paved with polychrome mosaic. Here is a glimpse into the lives of upper class Romans in the last sane interval before the western empire slid down into catastrophe. Gentili, to whom we are indebted for the largest share in the rebirth of this artistic treasure house, has reproduced possibly the finest sequences, the Great and Small Hunts. In these we see ostriches being loaded at a North African port, a wounded lioness turning on a huntsman, a captured boar being brought in, slung from a pole, and many other episodes of the chase. In general the mosaics are adapted to the rooms they adorn; thus the nurseries have a juvenile hunting scene in which a child captures a duck with his lasso, another has fallen down and is being attacked by the little animal he has been pursuing and yet another is being pecked by the cock that has turned on him. Everything here is in miniature, reminding us of the nursery rhyme tiles in our childhood bathrooms; where the grown-up quarters have the most elaborate representation yet discovered of chariot racing in a circus, the children have their own little circus with juvenile charioteers driving pairs of geese, flamingoes, plovers and wood pigeons. The species of bird are carefully chosen to represent the colours of the four factions of the Circus Maximus in Rome, respectively white, red, blue and green. The *factio prasina*, or "greens", are winning, and the little driver is about to be presented with the palm of victory. It must be more than coincidence that the same faction is winning in the "senior" circus at the other end of the palace; were the factions already political parties at this time, and did the Emperor support the greens?

The bikini girls, in the Room of the Ten Maidens, is the best known of the mosaics and the least artistic. The subjects, possibly taking part in an athletic contest or merely enacting one for the frivolous displays of the late Roman theatre, are not remarkable for feature or figure; one can see as good at Mondello Lido, near Palermo, on any day of the week, and better on Sundays. In extenuation is the fact that this mosaic floor was laid above the original one and at a later date, so that we are looking at examples of a debased art which has nothing in common with that of the rest of the villa.

In dating the palace, archaeologists relied partly on tiles and small objects that came to light. The style of the mosaics is identical with that of several Roman remains in North Africa which are usually dated to the last decade of the third century; it is so individual, moreover, that one can be fairly certain that North African artists were brought to Sicily to perform the actual work. Floor tiles have also been dated to the second half of the third century, and small objects unearthed, especially lamps and coins, are said to point to a date very shortly before Constantine.

Fashions were apt to change frequently at this time, and these were also used for accurate dating. Of the few fragments of statues that have survived, one foot wears an openwork shoe of the style seen on the porphyry group of the tetrarchs outside Saint Mark's in Venice. The statues represent the two Augusti embracing their Caesars and are obviously portraits taken from life; the low, cylindrical headgear, the "bobbed" hair and short beards of this group all appear in the mosaics of Piazza Armerina, for instance in the scene of the Great Hunt, where a dignified figure, leaning on a Tau staff, watches the proceedings. The staff, to digress for a moment, comes from ancient Egypt, and even before being adopted as the emblem of Saint Anthony Abbott was credited with magical powers. Among the female portraits are several that show the hair style prevailing at the time of the tetrarchs, which can be verified from an existing portrait of Diocletian's daughter Valeria, wife of the Caesar Galerius. All these facts suggested that the villa had belonged to one of the tetrarchs, and this was corroborated by further evidence.

In the division of spheres of influence Maximian retained Italy and North Africa, so that a hunting lodge convenient to both could well be sought in Sicily. Furthermore, one is struck by the frequency with which the ivy leaf (Latin *hedera*) appears as a decoration, especially on the clothes of some of the figures. By this time the *hedera*, with its initial H, had become the badge of the Herculean clan, and this is further emphasized by the space devoted to Hercules, including his apotheosis, among the mosaics. There is something pitiful about the rulers of the world when they reveal their eagerness for social standing, an ambition by no means confined to the time of the tetrarchs. Diocletian, son of slaves, adopted Jupiter as patron and consequently coined the family name Jovius; at the same time Maximian elected for Hercules and tacked the new name of Herculius to the Marcus Aurelius Valerius Maximianus, with about the same entitlement, considering his peasant origin. Apart from a colossal marble head of Hercules whose features, if we except the absent nose, are said to be those of Maximian, there are other portraits that strengthen the supposition. Near the baths is a portrait of a matron taking her two children to the baths, accompanied by two servant girls. The mother's hair style, combed back with ears uncovered, then brought forward and piled on top of the head, is typical of the age of the tetrarchs and duplicates that of Diocletian's wife Prisca, as seen carved oı a jewel. Her features include a crooked nose, present also on the son's face which shows an additional peculiarity, an inequality of the eyes; this is not, as sometimes stated, due to a triangular tessera being used for the left eye, instead of a square one, but to the fact that no black tessera at all is used for the left pupil.

If we now visit the so-called Vestibule of Eros and Pan, diagonally across the peristyle, we see the representation of their mythical fight, a common subject in ancient art. Among the audience are a boy and a girl, whose features are in all essentials the same as those of the other group except that in this one the boy's left eye has a pronounced squint. This, according to historians, was one of the distinguishing features of Maximian's son Maxentius, the same who accompanied the Milvian bridge into the Tiber after Constantine had won the battle of Saxa Rubra. Some of the mythical subjects are also meant to be taken personally; thus Maximian's successful campaign in North Africa is symbolized by the adventure of Hercules and the apples of the Hesperides, that of his assistant Constantius Chlorus by the defeated British rebel Carausius at the feet, once more, of Hercules.

6   The Heirs of Rome

Those were critical days in the rise of Christianity. The shadows of two great forces, deemed destructive by some, rejuvenating by others, loomed over the Roman Empire. About twenty years previously a prolonged raid by the Franks, the first of the barbarian incursions, had sacked and almost depopulated Syracuse; Christianity was the second threat and had already gained a large number of adherents in the island. An old tradition asserts that both Peter and Paul were among the saints who trod Sicilian ground, and though the latter was almost certainly a visitor, on his way to Rome from Malta, there is little to support the belief concerning the former. The first bishop of Syracuse, Saint Marcian, had been martyred and was buried where Saint Paul had preached two centuries earlier, during the stay of three days mentioned in the Acts. A long period of darkness separates Paul and Marcian, broken only by Saint Pantaenus, an historical character and teacher of Saint Clement of Alexandria; he did much to combat paganism in the island and is affectionately known as the "Sicilian bee", the Italian version of which—*l'Ape sicula*—is here given as a warning to the unwary.

As usual, it is difficult to know where tradition ceases and history begins. Messina dedicates its cathedral to the Madonna of the Letter in accordance with the legend (we cannot call it more than that) that the inhabitants wrote to the Virgin requesting that she place them under her protection and received a written affirmative reply. The letter itself is called *Il Graffeo*, a name given also to a Byzantine painting of the Madonna kept in the church of La Cattolica; strangely, it is not credited to Saint Luke, for this is the favourite attribution of all early, and even some late Byzantine Madonnas, but there used to be one in the cathedral that was allegedly his work, with which the visitor could console himself. Saint Lucy, who was martyred at Syracuse, probably during the persecution of Diocletian, is assigned a number of improbable adventures. Because of the similarity of the name *Lucia* and *luce* (light) she is invoked in ophthalmic disease and is often represented in the unsavoury role of carrying two eyes on a plate. Saint Agatha again, whose veil is inherited from Isis and can stop Etna's streams of lava, is the virgin martyr of Catania and somewhat senior to Lucy. Though she suffered many other vexations she is chiefly remembered for having her breasts cut off and outdoes Lucy by carrying them on a dish. Ignorant of morbid anatomy, well-intentioned artists portrayed them as dome-shaped, whence they became confused with bells and loaves so that the young martyr not only understandably became the patron saint of nursing mothers, but of bell founders too, and also has loaves of bread blessed in some churches on 5th February, her feast day.

San Calogero is a Sicilian saint with a singular origin. Officially he is stated to have come from Chalcedon, opposite Constantinople, in the fifth century; he lived in various districts, particularly those now known as Marsala and Sciacca, and died on Mount Cronios of the latter district, whence it has been renamed Monte Calogero. He was a hermit, with a face as black as ebony, and patron of the town of Naro in the sulphur mining part of central Sicily. He and other new immigrants were no longer called by the Aramaic title *Abba*, but by the Greek words *kalos geron*, literally "noble old man"; the new word *calogero* was thus evolved to signify a hermit and hundreds of years later, when monks came from Mount Athos to make the mosaics of Cefalù, they were still called *calogeri*. So it is possible that Saint Calogero represents a dim memory of an eastern hermit with a dark skin, who displaced a pagan tutelary deity on Mount Cronios—the name suggests it might have been sacred to the father of Zeus—and brought his worship into the catholic embrace of the early church.

When Rome and the western world went down before successive waves of Goths, Vandals, Franks, Herulians, Lombards and other Teutonic tribes, Byzantium in the east survived. Long ago Constantine had realized that Rome's situation had little to recommend it, administratively or strategically, and had transformed the old town of Byzantium into his new capital, Constantinople.

The new rulers in the west, with or without the support of the popes, ensured that the enmity with Byzantium would be religious as well as territorial. In spite of the sufferings of Sicily under the barbarian Arians, we know that the island remained in the Western Church from the fact that Pope Leo I consulted Pascasino, Bishop of Lilybaeum, with regard to fixing the proper date for Easter, in the year 440. Even after the Byzantine conquest the Roman Church retained a considerable hold, as is shown by the protective interest of Gregory the Great, whose mother Sylvia was, as I have said, a Sicilian heiress.

The Byzantine emperors seem to have done little for the country during 300 years' rule; such remains as exist are modest and often consist of second-rate alterations to existing structures [*opposite*]. And yet, for a brief period, Sicily's capital became that of the Byzantine Empire. Accounts differ as to why Constans II left Constantinople; some say that he was disgusted with the perpetual intrigue of the court and stopped at Syracuse on his way to Rome, where he wanted to revive the ancient glory. Others affirm that his villainies made Constantinople too hot to hold him. Both versions would fit the story that he spat from his galley against the walls of the city he was abandoning. It is certain that he lived in Syracuse from 662 to 668, after a destructive raid through southern Italy, and that his avarice

TINDARI—Greco-Byzantine Tower

did not stop at stealing church plate. His ring is the only tangible link with him that we have, but the manner of his death presents, as Sherlock Holmes would have put it, several features of interest.

This brings us to the mystery of the soap dish. Tired of Constans and his behaviour, a courtier is said to have killed him in the Baths of Daphne in Syracuse by hitting him on the head with a soap dish. The story, admittedly not told by the best authorities, is intriguing. Has anyone seen a Byzantine soap dish? Did the Byzantines use soap? To the second question, probably "yes" for clothes and "no" for bathing. So far as I know, the classical procedure was still used: increasingly hot rooms, then a cold plunge, the rub with olive oil (to save unnecessary expense only the third pressing was used) and finally the scraping with the *strigil*, as portrayed in the well-known Apoxyomenos statue in the Vatican Museum. The accepted story, and the one used by Gibbon, is that a servant, having poured water over him at the baths, hit him on the head with the vase and let him drown while unconscious. Scaturro relates the episode in far more satisfactory detail: on 15th July, 668, he says, a courtier named Andrew son of Troilus, while anointing the emperor, emptied a jug of boiling water over him and finished him off by hitting him on the head with the bronze vessel. The same story is told by Maggiore, who lived over a hundred years before Scaturro and can therefore be absolved from collusion. The point is a trivial one but I feel strongly about the Soap Dish Heresy.

Though the architectural and artistic influence of Byzantium was halted by the Arab conquest of the ninth century, it returned with renewed vigour 200 years later. At this juncture I shall refer only to a few of the meagre evidences of their domination from 535 to 827, to give the traditional dates; I mention this because conquests take time and there were many years at both ends of this period when Byzantine rule was only partial. What records we have also show that it was unpopular; taxes were high and hence the economy suffered from the necessity of concentrating on cash crops that give a quick return. In this way the great olive plantations, a legacy of the Greeks, were neglected in favour of wheat and vines, and an additional impetus was given to soil erosion. The same sequence has been seen in our own generation in Africa, where cash crops like cotton have taken precedence over legumes and other plants more beneficial to the soil. According to Tomeucci—I must add this, though I know there is nothing so boring as other people's finances—the textile and salt fish industries died out at the same time and for the same reason. It seems fár more likely that they were deliberately suppressed to protect two well-known home industries of Constantinople.

Little attention is paid to the occasional relic of the Byzantine era. The southern city walls of Agrigento are honeycombed with their niche graves, emptied of every scrap of their contents. The National Gallery in Palermo displays a few fragments of decorative architecture, including the very typical vine meander on marble door jambs, as adopted by the Visigoths in Spain; the best examples, however, can be seen in the same city, in the twelfth century Church of Saint Anthony Abbott.

Centuries of neglect have not quite obliterated the many tiny churches—the Italian use the pretty diminutive *chiesette*—which dotted the country in early Christian and Byzantine days. One of the most instructive, as well as pathetic in its present state, is the one which lies nearest to Santa Croce di Camerina, in the Province of Ragusa [*Col. pl. V(a)*]. To find it you have to take an earth road running south-west from the town, asking every passer-by whether he knows the *cuba*; this is the traditional Sicilian name for any old domed building, the word being derived from the Arabic *kubbeh*. At about one mile you will see the little dome rising out of the ploughed earth or waving crops about a hundred yards off the road on your left.

Nothing quite like it is to be seen elsewhere. The dome, made of heavy, roughly shaped blocks, rests on the square structure by means of pendentives; for the uninstructed, these are a device by which a square building can take a round dome, whose weight is fairly evenly distributed, instead of resting only on the centre of each wall. Even so, the centre is the weakest part of the wall and probably for this reason was reinforced by apses, which act as buttresses. The Romans, as we saw at Piazza Armerina, used this scheme and often placed statues in the apses; in the early church the central apse was used for the altar. The entrance, opposite, has a primitive porch whose barrel-vaulted roof rather surprisingly runs transversely. From inside you will see how the addition of the porch has transformed a square building into the shape of a Latin cross, with one long arm, the standard shape of all mediaeval and later churches. Working out the ground plan entails dropping into the interior, which is now about five feet below ground level, and a good deal of grubbing about. Of all the early Christian and Byzantine churches of Sicily this, with its primitive clover-leaf plan, is the most stirring; though it is not, as so often stated, based on the same plan as Hagia Sophia, the contrast between the humble, twelve by twelve foot buried church of Santa Croce di Camerina and the opulent splendour of the Constantinople masterpiece is a poignant one and I have no doubt which one the Saviour would have chosen for His devotions.

The trouble with these early churches is the difficulty in finding them. The *cuba* is comparatively easy compared with the Cupola di Malvagna, near Francavilla; to get to this a guide must be found—I was fortunate enough to have a student recommended by the parish priest—and a cross-country walk with considerable obstacles performed. The building, only slightly larger than the *cuba*, is also domed and built on the same plan; being used to house a cistern it is rather better preserved, but the inquiring visitor will see where the original door, curiously placed in the east wall, has been built up and replaced by a modern entrance through one of the apses.

The last and biggest is the abandoned Church of Santa Domenica, situated below and visible from the charming hill town of Castiglione di Sicilia, itself worth a visit. Before descending to the plain, therefore, finding the path which crosses the railway line at the correct place and trudging along the narrow lane with its high stone walls that leads to Santa Domenica, it is worth while strolling round this old strong-point and absorbing its mediaeval atmosphere. The Church of San Pietro has a most ingenious interior sundial, whereby a ray of light enters through a hole in the south wall at precisely midday and falls on a marble strip in the floor; the date can be deduced from the spot where the strip is illuminated, varying as it does with the height of the sun. The interior of Santa Domenica, alas, has nothing so elegant to show, for it is shamefully used as a cowshed. From outside can be seen the remains of biforate and triforate windows, that is with the window space divided by one or two slender columns, the characteristic dome and the striped voussoirs of black lava, red volcanic stone and white marble in the arches [below]. The windows, dome and arch, when encountered elsewhere, are invariably cited as proving the Arab origin of a building; this church alone should be sufficient to refute such over-simplification, for it dates from well before the Arab conquest. It might as well be stated here that it was from the Byzantines that the Arabs took over all the above architectural features, along with yashmaks, eunuchs and other aids to gracious living. The loss of Sicily to the Arabs by no means ended Byzantine interest or influence, politically or artistically; the second flowering, which took place after the Norman conquest, has left legacies which make up in artistic mastery for what they lack in emotional appeal.

7   The Sons of the Prophet

"The loss of Sicily was occasioned by an act of superstitious rigour. An amorous youth, who had stolen a nun from her cloister, was sentenced by the Emperor to the amputation of his tongue. Euphemius appealed to the reason and policy of the Saracens of Africa..." And this, according to Gibbon, is why the Byzantines lost Sicily. The real story is of course more complicated, for Islam had been carried at the sword-point over an area stretching from central Asia to the Atlantic and was still expanding its territory at the beginning of the ninth century. Sicily under the Byzantines had been repeatedly raided from North Africa, and we may be sure that by 827 the Aghlabites ("Conquerors") of Tunis, successors to the territory and ambitions of the Carthaginians, were waiting for the opportunity to invade Sicily. Here again we see how it was to form the central of three bridges for the Moslem invasion of Europe. In the same century the Moslem menace was felt in every part of the Mediterranean, and Rome itself was attacked twice by North African Saracens who succeeded in despoiling the churches of Saint Peter and Saint Paul, both of which were outside the existing fortifications; in 884 the Abbey of Monte Cassino was completely destroyed, neither for the first nor the last time.

The raids had been going on since 652, when Othman of Damascus had mounted an unsuccessful attack, being routed by Olympus, exarch of Ravenna and representative of a still powerful Eastern Roman Empire. As late as 820 the raids had become so insupportable that an almost forgotten military genius, Count Boniface of Corsica, repeated the strategy of Agathocles and Scipio and attacked the Arab possessions in North Africa. The manoeuvre was successful once more and the Arab troops, who had already established themselves in Sicily, were recalled to defend their homeland; we may be sure that they brought back with them tales of the lovely island they had set out to conquer. Seven years after this little known episode came the real invasion.

Squabbles and treachery played their usual part in the fall of Christian Sicily, which began in the ninth century. The Moslems who landed at Mazara in 827 were a mixed lot. The choice of this riverain port depended partly on the presence of many supporters of Euphemius, who had to wear a wild plant in their helmet to distinguish them from hostile Byzantines, and partly on the powerful and deadly defences of Lilybaeum; this harbour would have been preferable for every reason, whence its later name of Marsala, as I have explained. At Mazara were landed Moslems of every colour and nationality, Arabs and Berbers, especially Howâra tribesmen, Persians from Khorassan and refugees from Spain. The last, incidentally, settled in the western part of Sicily and this possibly accounts for the presence of majolica lustre ware in Palermo, indistinguishable from the beautiful products of Hispano-Moresque potteries. When the invasion fleet sailed from Susa, just south of Cape Bon, it was under the command of Asad ibn at-Furàt, a pious and learned Mesopotamian; others say that the leader was called Halcam or Adelcamo, who committed unheard of barbarities (they must have been pretty bad to astonish the Byzantines) and eventually built himself a castle on Mount Bonifacio, where now the little town of Alcamo is named after him. The conquest of Sicily was by no means assured by the establishment of a footing in western Sicily, and one is struck by the slow progress made by the Moslems. The landing at Mazara was in 827; Palermo fell in 831 and became the new capital of the island, Castrogiovanni (Enna) in 859, Syracuse in 878 and Taormina in 902. Even then the Byzantines prolonged the fight until 965 and less than a century later, in 1038, their brilliant general George Maniakes almost succeeded in reconquering the island; it is probable that he would have done so had not his initial successes aroused the usual fear and jealousy in the royal bosom at Constantinople and led to his recall.

The fact is that the Moslems, though they were good fighters, often ably led and welcomed by a substantial part of the population, were handicapped almost from the start by continuous quarrels. They thus repeated in miniature the whole history of the great Arab conquests, which might well have established mastery over most of Europe, had there been harmony among their leaders. The details of their squabbles are unedifying and unimportant; it is enough to remember that Sicily was an Aghlabite dependency for about a hundred years and that, when the Fatimids took over from that dynasty, an emirate based on Palermo exerted whatever control there was over the island. At this stage, when Palermo was allegedly resplendent with 500 mosques and rivalled Córdoba and Cairo in magnificence, only lip-service was paid to the Fatimid caliph and there was a perfunctory mention of his name during Friday prayers.

Moslem rule was an improvement over that of Byzantium. The *latifondi* were divided among freed serfs and smallholders, and agriculture received the greatest impetus it had ever known. Thanks to a Moslem custom, uncultivated land became the property of whoever first broke it, thus encouraging cultivation at the expense of grazing. Practically all the distinguishing features of Sicilian husbandry were introduced by the Arabs: citrus, cotton, carob, mulberry—both the *celso*, or black and the white *morella*—sugar cane, hemp, date palm, the list is almost endless. Saffron apparently owes its continued popularity to its alleged aphrodisiac property, but is not to everyone's taste; Goethe, for instance, complained that the chicken and rice he was served in Catania was inedible from an excess of saffron, while the only other feature of the city that he considered noteworthy was the huge and wonderful organ in the Church of Saint Nicholas, made by the appropriately named Donato del Piano. Though, as previously mentioned, papyrus may have been introduced by the daughter of a Ptolemy, it was the Arabs who first used it as writing material. Syracuse, by the way, is by no means the only place where papyrus has flourished. In Moslem times it grew in that quarter of Palermo which is still called *Papireto*, in what was called "the dirty spring", from the fact that their women used to congregate there to wash their hair. It is very likely that they also introduced lucerne which, under one Arabic name, came to Spain and America as *alfalfa*; in Sicily it is still called by another, *sudda* or "flower of the *sudd*". Mention of the great, tropical swamp along the upper reaches of the Nile brings us back to papyrus, for Benjamin of Tudela, that intrepid twelfth-century traveller, described this in his Hebrew diary as the "*sadd*" of Palermo, using the same word that was translated as "flags" in the Authorized Version of the second chapter of Exodus; in the New English Bible it is more accurately rendered as "reeds".

When the Fatimids succeeded the Aghlabites at about the middle of the tenth century, Sicily became practically independent, being ruled by an emir whose capital was at Palermo. Under him were three provincial *cadis* whose territories, the *wali*, survive today in the Val di Mazara, Val di Noto and the Val Demone, respectively the western, south-eastern and north-eastern thirds of the island. Towns which had surrendered to the invaders retained their nominal independence on payment of tribute, though attempts at converting the Sicilians to Islam, in accordance with the Koranic precept, persisted. One of the more reasonable aspects of Moslem rule was the fact that the offspring of a believer and a Christian captive was legitimate and not stigmatized; this fact, added to the large scale conversion in the western half of Sicily, accounts for the persistence of Arab features, especially in the Val di Mazara, to this day.

The most obvious reminders of two centuries of Arab rule are several hundred place-names. Those beginning with "Calta-" are invariably derived from *qa'lat*, a citadel; thus Caltabellotta is *qa'lat ab-bellut* (as nearly as it can be transliterated), meaning "citadel of the oaks" and Caltanisetta perpetuates the ancient town of Nissa through *qa'lat-nissa*. We found the word for "harbour" in Marsala; wandering along the coast off the beaten track reveals tiny fishing villages with names such as Marzamemi (Marsa Mehmet?) and simple Marza, both near Cape Passaro; like many hamlets hereabouts they consist of gaily painted houses, pink, yellow, blue and green, that remind one of Burano in the lagoon of Venice. But even in everyday speech the Sicilian language preserves reminders of the Moslem past: they have a word *sciaccatu*, pronounced "shacatu", which has a Sicilian past participle tacked on to an Arabic word for "cracked" and is used much as in English slang; *zubbio*, a communal burial pit, is taken from the Arabic for a rubbish dump. The invocation at the division of corn, allegedly derived from Greek days, is only a literal translation of *Bismillah*, "in the name of God". And in many parts anything old is to this day attributed to the Moslems; along the north coast the olive trees grow to an impressive size, being called *saracinu, saracinescu*, or, with a fine disregard for chronology, *olivari di tò nannu*—planted by your grandfather.

To identify Saracen buildings in Sicily is to tread on dangerous ground, for the experts themselves agree on none. As in Spain, Moslem inhabitants carried out much of the building programme ordered by the later Christian conquerors, so that Arabic influence is obvious, though often blended in a pleasing fashion with Byzantine, Romanesque or even later styles. Most guide books refer to the modest baths of Cefalà Diana as the only undoubted Saracen building that survives; two others are worthy of mention. The first is really only the survival of a custom in the little town of Tindari, where each house has an outdoor oven exactly as in many parts of North Africa [*below*]. The other is a bridge, still called *Ponte dei Saraceni* in spite of experts' attribution to the fourteenth century [*opposite*]. It spans the Simeto River behind Etna and takes some finding, but the quest is rewarding, whether you believe in its Saracen or mediaeval origin. The bridge lies about five miles north-west of the town of Adrano, where the principal church uses sixteen antique columns that may have come from the temple where the miracle of the sweating god was observed (Chapter 4). To find the bridge, stay on the east bank of the river and go upstream along

whatever vile track presents itself; it is useless to choose one which promises a fair surface, they are all bad. The bridge has four unequal arches with striped voussoirs, so you will not be confused by the great aqueduct of thirty-one arches built by Prince Biscari in 1761. This again may be of historical significance, for the other Sicily, that is the kingdom of Naples, benefited from the reforms introduced by the regent, Tanucci, during the minority of Ferdinand III, who came to the throne in 1759. Though Sicily itself did not share directly in this relief it may well be that the trend of the times was already making itself felt.

Dealing first with details of architecture, we find both guides and guide books only too eager to ascribe some of the commoner features of Sicilian decoration to Arab authorship. Admittedly, the type of dome which one sees best in Palermo, but also in out-of-the-way places such as Santa Trinità di Delia near Castelvetrano [*Col pl. VI*], is pure Arabic and can be identified by the cylindrical portion surmounted by the hemisphere, drum and dome in one, as it were. Of Arab origin, too, are the pierced stone or plaster windows, with their intricate geometric patterns, but one must also remember that similar *transennae* were a feature of Carolingian architecture and can today be seen in Aachen Cathedral and in the old church of Santa Sabina in Rome, where they date from the eighth and ninth centuries. The so-called Dark Ages were lighter than we used to believe, and there was a constant interchange of knowledge and ideas between the supposedly hostile worlds of the Cross and the Crescent. The Arabs were the greater borrowers, for they arrived on the stage of history as semi-nomads with no

architecture of their own; hence, with the exception of decorated surfaces, their buildings were modifications of Byzantine, Persian or western European designs.

The chevron, or zig-zag, provides an excellent example, for it decorates many a mediaeval Sicilian door and window. It is invariably adduced as a proof of Arabic workmanship, though we know exactly when and where it originated; "A second decorative motif, which appeared soon afterwards," * says Stoll, "rapidly became an important distinguishing characteristic of late English Romanesque. This was the chevron or zigzag, a motif whose fecundity was such that it spread virtually everywhere . . . and even travelled to Apulia and Sicily in the wake of the Normans." When used as a decoration on columns it appears in early mediaeval buildings, and sometimes even earlier, in widely separated parts of Europe. Apart altogether from Britain, where it can be seen from Dunfermline to Iffley, the cloister of San Paolo fuori le Mura in Rome, the portals of the abbey Church of Saint Denis in Paris and the Collegiate Church of Königslutter in Germany provide sufficient evidence. At Monreale, near Palermo, there is a so-called Moorish fountain in one corner of the beautiful Benedictine cloister [*opposite*]; the zigzag pattern is adduced as evidence of this absurd claim, which has nothing to support it except the slavish reiteration of generations of guides. The shape was one commonly used in the twelfth and thirteenth centuries—witness the Fontana Maggiore at Perugia—and the figures forming part of the ornamental summit of the column are quite unlike anything that Moslem artists would dare to produce, in view of Moslem prejudice against the portrayal of the human form; this prejudice, by the way, is not based on the Koran, but on the *Hadith*, or collection of Mohamed's sayings.

Buildings that are regarded as essentially Saracen, such as the Cubula of Palermo, a garden kiosk built for the Norman rulers by Moslem hands, have an interesting ancestry. They are related to the fire temples of Persia and the Buddhist *stupas* further east. Both were subjected to changes introduced by invaders from Central Asia.

The rule of Islam, with its necessary changes in language, religion, art and blood, could not simply be wiped out when new conquerors arrived, and indeed no serious effort was made to do so. To trace all the legacies of the Saracen occupation would require more space and knowledge than are at my disposal; a few have been mentioned but more omitted. When worshippers are described by Louise Caico as crawling along the church floor at Porta Atenea, near Agrigento, we are reminded of the saintly Rabi'ah, who dragged herself along the ground from 'Arafat to Mecca, and the same author noted that Sicilian country folk counted the time from sunset, as is done in most Islamic countries today. The coral hands that are still occasionally offered for sale are the Arab amulet against the Evil Eye, and

* i.e. soon after 1110.

Sicilian women who use their shawls to conceal all but one eye are unconsciously imitating the women of Andalucia, another European outpost of
Islam, in their custom of *taparse de medio ojo*. Copper or brass *bracieri*, in
which olive stones or almond shells are burned, are of roughly the same
shape as those used in Spain or the *kanoun* of Morocco and the *mangal* of
Anatolia, whose distant ancestor has been discovered in the remains of
Hittite settlements that flourished over two thousand years before Christ.

8   *The Northmen*

Every now and then an unknown hand throws a pebble into the puddle which we call the world and the ripples that spread in every direction mark the shock waves of its impact. Rome was such a one, Islam another. A third example was provided by the men of the North, the Norsemen, Normans, Vikings, Vaeringjar, raiders and traders, pirates and explorers. It is true that they were feared as much as, or more than the plague: "from the fury of the Northmen, good Lord, deliver us," said the old litany. But with all their brutality and destructiveness these pagans carried within them the seeds of greatness, respect for law, courage in battle and fortitude in adversity. Even after a thousand years their achievements rival those of any other nation: they colonized Iceland and Greenland, discovered the continent of North America, traded into the centre of Russia, which is named after them, sailed thence down the great rivers to the Caspian and Black Seas, and from that trading empire supplied a bodyguard for the Emperor of Constantinople. They carved out homelands in Normandy, after sailing up the Seine and sacking Paris, and in southern Italy. At second remove they founded kingdoms in England and Sicily and set up their rule or authority in North Africa, Greece and the Near East. With incredible boldness and matchless effrontery they established trading posts and pirate bases at the mouth of almost every sizeable river of Europe from the Baltic to the South of France. Though overpopulation in Scandinavia undoubtedly began the centrifugal movement, when large parts of France and the British Isles were conquered by Vikings, it cannot account for the enormous expansion that followed the comparatively small expeditions that set out from home. Had land been all that was needed, they would surely have been content to settle for longer in the rich lands they had conquered, as did every other Teutonic nation that took part in the great migrations of the Dark Ages.

The urge for the ripple to spread, for trade and plunder to be sought in ever more distant parts, was combined with a natural capacity to rule and a genius for assimilation. It is for this reason that Norman rule in Sicily attained an excellence hitherto unknown in the island. Southern Italy, at the beginning of the eleventh century, provided a battlefield for a number of rival nations. The Byzantine Greeks had held Apulia and other parts since the days of Belisarius; the Lombards, their former allies, had carved out for themselves a southern kingdom, centred on Benevento; the Holy Roman

Emperor had designs on the whole of Italy, the Pope was anxious to increase the Papal States at almost anyone's expense; independent coastal cities, such as Gaeta and Amalfi, held precariously to their trade and Saracen raiders clung to the flanks of Italy like hounds round a wounded boar.

Into this bewildering tangle of enmities and alliances entered forty Norman pilgrims in the year 1016. The news travelled back to the Seine and a continuous dribble of reinforcements, chiefly younger sons and squires, came to join their cousins until their numbers made them a power to be reckoned with. But this time the Northmen did not come as traders; all that they could offer for sale were their swords and bodies, and it was thus that they first set foot in Sicily.

By this time Arab rule in Sicily had followed the general trend; as their ties with the caliphs grew more tenuous their solidarity weakened proportionately and civil war broke out. In 1035 a fresh force of 6,000, led by Abdallah, son of the Zirid Caliph of Kairouan, joined in the turmoil on the side of Abu Hafs, who was in revolt against his brother, the Emir of Palermo. The latter appealed for help to Byzantium and though he was promptly assassinated, sufficient excuse had been provided for a Byzantine attempt to regain their rule over Sicily. The brilliant George Maniakes was chosen to command the invasion force, consisting of Greeks, Bulgarians, Lombards and Italians; calling at Salerno to collect a contribution from the Lombard Prince Gaimar, he picked up a few hundred Normans, dissatisfied with the outbreak of unaccustomed peace. These, together with a contingent of Varangians, under Harald Hardrada, would provide the shock troops of the Greek army. It would be thirty years before the bold, much travelled Harald met his death at Stamford Bridge at the hands of Saxon Harold, himself destined shortly to fall before other Northmen.

The expedition of Maniakes, which had succeeded in recovering the eastern half of Sicily, failed from the usual internal causes. His unpopularity led to the story that he coveted the throne of Sicily; this was a certain way of achieving the downfall of any competent general, from Belisarius onward, and Maniakes was recalled and imprisoned, while Sicily reverted to Moslem rule. But the expedition had achieved its purpose; during the siege of Syracuse, one William de Hauteville earned the title of *Bras-de-fer* by his feat in unhorsing and killing the emir in a sudden charge. "Iron arm" was a real compliment among the hardy Normans, one of whom had felled a horse with a single blow of his fist, without earning a nickname. The statement that the Norman knights owed their superiority to the use of stirrups cannot remain unchallenged; the history of the stirrup is of great interest, not least because of the delay before it was adopted by the Romans, but the belief that it was unknown to the Arabs requires revision, for it is certainly pictured in an eighth century wall painting in the Syrian castle of Kasr al-Hair.

William *Bras-de-fer* was only the eldest, but by no means the most remarkable, of the twelve sons of Tancred de Hauteville, whose small estate lay near Coutances. The last seven were produced by Tancred's second wife, Fressenda, and of these the first, Robert, and the last, Roger, were the conquerors of Sicily. William and the other Normans who had campaigned there under George Maniakes must have brought back many a tale of the beauty, and particularly the wealth and fertility, of Sicily; twenty years later the chronic dissensions of the Arabs gave them the chance for which they had been waiting. The Hautevilles, among whom Robert Guiscard was the most astute, now turned their attention to Sicily, and in their usual methodical way conquered it piecemeal.

Palermo held out until 1072, though as early as 1068 the Saracens had sustained the decisive defeat of Misilmeri after which Ayub fled back to Africa with the remains of his troops. From J. J. Norwich we have the instructive tale of how the Normans captured baskets of carrier pigeons, whose use had long been forgotten in Europe though not in the East, and how Roger ordered that they should be released after a scrap of material dyed with Saracen blood had been attached to the leg of each as a primitive form of psychological warfáre. The Normans appear to have had some difficulty in finding suitable camping grounds around the Conca d'Oro in which Palermo lies, and one of the hill tops was the site of a painful and somewhat humiliating infestation with spiders. It is tempting to take the present village of Altavilla Milicia as the descendant of one of their camps, for the remains of a church built by Guiscard himself flank the new *autostrada* and the name, as I pointed out to a surprised inhabitant, is only the Italian for Hauteville.

Crusade or no crusade, the Normans were too shrewd to allow racial or religious considerations to interfere with their conquest. A hundred years later Christians and Saracens were living side by side, amicably enough, but both with cause to complain that their co-religionists were tending to apostasize. Thus, in a deed of gift to the Church made by one Robert of Golisano in 1183, ten serfs are included, some of them featuring in this extract: "... Philip son of Bulfadar. Basil son of Abdesseid. These are Christians. Saracens are Hasem son of Themen, Omor son of Dahamen ..." Tolerance and adaptability were the two peculiarly Norman qualities that made the kingdom of Sicily one of the most brilliant of its time.

The royal succession in Norman Sicily can be reduced to four essential rulers: Roger I, brother of Robert Guiscard, assumed the title "Grand Count of Sicily" in 1072, declared his independence in 1091 and died in 1101. His son, Roger II, was the first to be crowned, and changed his title from Count to King in 1130; the Normans were adept at aiding, opposing and even capturing popes at the right time, and Roger ruled Sicily as apostolic legate long before his coronation. He was thus entitled to wear mitre, dalmatic and sandals and carry the pastoral crook, as in the celebrated mosaic from the Church of the Martorana in Palermo [*Col. pl. VII (b and c)*]. William I, called "The Bad"—by his enemies of course—reigned for only twelve years and was succeeded by his son William II, a pleasant nonentity who allowed prelates and barons to have much their own way and thus earned the title of "The Good". He died in 1189, and with him perished the remarkable multinational civilization of the Normans. I have thought it as well to list the important kings, as I remember the horror of a student at seeing the street called Ruggero Settimo, in Palermo. "Seven Rogers," he moaned, obviously convinced that the first two were enough for any historian to bear. His fears were vain for Settimo, a surname and not a number, was president of the short-lived first free Sicilian parliament in 1845, before Garibaldi's liberation of the island in 1860.

True to their Norman ancestry, the kings regarded their pleasant island as a bridge for further conquests. Roger II won a foothold in North Africa and William the Bad lost it. Both of them ventured east and made conquests at the expense of the Byzantines; thus the former, largely through the exertions of his admiral, George of Antioch, took Malta, Corfu and Cephalonia, whence he could conduct the usual piratical raids on the mainland of Greece. Among his conquests were Thebes and Corinth which, with their classical memories, seem strangely out of place in a Norman chronicle, in much the same way as does the Duke of Athens in *A Midsummer Night's Dream*. The most valuable booty won in this campaign were the silk weavers of both sexes whom George of Antioch transported forcibly to Sicily, where they set up a flourishing industry.

Roger II, perhaps with memories of his Viking ancestors, was the founder of a large and efficient navy which made these conquests possible. The greatest of their naval admirals was Margaritus of Bari, who has sometimes been confused with Margaret, the king's mother, so that I have even read the absurd statement that a woman admiral defeated Saladin's navy during the third crusade, in 1188.

Life at the Norman court must have been colourful. We read of eunuchs occupying important posts, as in Byzantium, and a certain Richard styled Gaytus, the Latin version of *caid*. Roger II, and some of his successors, travelled in considerable state with a bodyguard of Saracens and their own harem, though whitewashers of a later age maintain that the women were Arab sempstresses who embroidered Christian texts in Arabic lettering on the king's ceremonial robes. Not, one would think, a full-time job. Benjamin of Tudela, that remarkable traveller, describes the Palermo of those days, and its 1,500 Jewish families. His most profound impression seems to have been the royal palace and gardens, adapted from those of Saracen times, and the lake with boats "in which the king takes pleasure trips with his women". As King William II was sixteen at the time it is as well for censors of morals that he was nick-named "The Good".

To reconstruct the daily life at the king's court is almost impossible. A haven for scholars of all races and religions, al-Edrisi the geographer, Abelard of Bath the scientist, mosaicists from Greece, Cistercians and

Benedictines jostled each other in the corridors, waiting to receive suggestions for their part in beautifying the realm or increasing the sum of human knowledge. Roger II spoke and wrote Arabic and his son William I earned the title *"fortissimus"*, for he could straighten with his hands two horseshoes put together and lift a loaded pack animal; his father called him Fortinbras, or Strong i' th' arm and we can well believe that people were terrified when they saw him for the first time, with black beard and scowling features, doing his daily dozen with a pack mule.

Though Sicily was a favourite place of embarkation for crusaders, there was no sign of intolerance at this time; Ibn Jubair remarked on the contentment of the Moslems and was surprised to see the Christian women going veiled out of doors, adding that they never stopped talking. The same crusaders often fell under the spell of the orient when they had established a foothold in Syria, as did the warriors of the short-lived crusade of Barbastro in Spain. However barbaric the methods of warfare may have been, though Heaven knows that we are in no position to pass judgement, total warfare was still unknown and civilians of either side could travel without hindrance through each others' territory. Thus Moslem geographers could pass through large parts of Christian Europe, and Saint Francis of Assisi could undertake a goodwill mission to the Sultan Malek al-Kamel in 1219, while war was raging between Islam and the Cross. It seems as if this happy and civilized concept of the civilian's freedom persisted until the days of Napoleon.

Just as Sicily can show more classical Greek remains than can Greece itself, so do Norman remains outnumber those of other countries. Wherever you go, especially in the poorer parts of the interior, you come across Norman churches and castles; for here as elsewhere poverty is the best method of preserving mediaeval remains, while wealth destroys them with baroque restoration. A few mediaeval bridges still exist—we shall see one in Palermo—but beware of following the guide book too slavishly. The one across the Alcantara, near Francavilla, was blown up by the retreating Germans in the last war and has been rebuilt in modern style, but its mediaeval ghost still haunts guide books written in the last few years. The castle of Maniace, built by Margaret, mother of William II, marks the site of a settlement founded by George Maniakes during his partial conquest of Sicily, allegedly after a victory here by Harald Hardrada; its subsequent history is equally romantic and today it remains the headquarters of the dukedom of Bronte, the estate bestowed on Horatio Nelson and still the property of his heirs.

Norman architecture in Sicily is unique in its blend of east and west. Pointed arches, of Saracen origin, surmount Romanesque portals decorated with chevrons, and Saracen cupolas surmount a church in which windows may show the shallow, receding arches of a Byzantine building, as at Santa Trinità di Delia, near Castelvetrano [*Col. pl. VI*]. This seemingly endless variety is surely one of Sicily's greatest charms; compared with the austere buildings of the north, uniform in style and execution, such mixtures as the Norman church of San Biagio on the foundations of a Greek temple (*see also page 37*), or a similar adaptation of a pre-existing mosque, as we shall find at San Giovanni degli Eremiti, give us the exotic stone counterpart of the multiracial society of those distant days.

The end of the Norman kingdom coincided roughly with that of the twelfth century. William II and Joanna, daughter of England's Henry II, produced no children and after his death she was imprisoned by Tancred, illegitimate cousin of her husband, who also attempted to retain her dowry contrary to custom. But her brother, Richard Coeur-de-lion, stopped at Messina on his way to the third crusade, inflicted as much damage as he could on the innocent inhabitants, succeeded in liberating his sister and, more important, recovering her dowry. The money came in useful for, as everyone will remember from his school days, Richard was captured by the Holy Roman Emperor, Henry VI, on his way home from the crusade and had to purchase his liberty for an enormous sum. Joanna had meanwhile married Raymond VI of Toulouse, the same who defied the Pope by siding with his heretical Albigensian subjects and, during the crusade which probably shed more innocent blood than any other, a record hard to achieve, was excommunicated and reconciled with monotonous frequency.

While William was still alive a marriage had been arranged, largely at the instigation of Archbishop Walter of Palermo and against the Pope's wishes, between William's aunt Constance and Henry of Hohenstaufen, son of the Emperor Barbarossa. The same Henry, on the death of his father during the second crusade, became Holy Roman Emperor in his turn and used Richard I's ransom to finance the invasion of Sicily, basing his claim to the throne on his wife's descent. Tancred having died in 1194, Henry came to terms with his widow Sibylla, promising to bestow a county on her young son William III; with characteristic brutality he blinded, castrated and imprisoned his youthful rival, repressed a Sicilian revolt with which his wife was said to be in sympathy, and died shortly afterwards, regretted by none. His burning alive of several hundred nobles who had attended Tancred's coronation was one of the milder of his atrocities.

In this way the struggle between Guelphs and Ghibellines, which was to bedevil Italy for centuries, came to Sicily. The Pope had always regarded himself as the feudal lord of Norman Sicily and had thus opposed Constance's marriage to the Swabian Henry of Hohenstaufen, destined to become leader of the Ghibellines. Here we see the origin of the long struggle between successive Popes and the remarkable son, born to Constance in her forties, who was to be known as "The Wonder of the World".

9 *The Wonder of the World*

"*Hohenstaufen*, Frederick Roger von. *b.* 1194, in public, at Jesi, Ancona, to Constance d.o. Roger II of Sicily, and Henry VI, Holy Roman Emperor or, alternatively, an incubus. *Educ.* Privately and by ostlers, gamekeepers and Moslems in the markets of Palermo. *Honours:* King of the Romans, 1195; King of Sicily, 1198; Holy Roman Emperor 1215; King of Jerusalem, 1225, etc. etc. *m.* (1) Constance of Aragon, 1209; (2) Yolande of Jerusalem, 1225; (3) Isabella of England, 1235; (4) (probably) Bianca Lancia. *Children:* numerous, some legitimate. *Professions:* government, legality. *Relig.* Roman Catholic, own brand, whenever not excommunicated. *Publ. Liber Augustalis, De arte venandi cum avibus*, etc. *Hobbies:* Philosophy, mathematics, poetry, zoology, hunting, falconry. *Clubs:* Teutonic Order, Crusaders'."

Thus runs the entry in my imaginary mediaeval *Who's Who* for one of the most remarkable men that ever lived, a Renaissance ruler two centuries before his time, a man whose achievements perished in a world of ignorance while his ideas survived for an age of enlightenment; Frederick II, who enters with a flourish of trumpets and leaves with the designation of his contemporary Matthew Paris: *Stupor mundi et immutator mirabilis*— wonder of the world and marvellous innovator. It is impossible to do more than touch on his adventures outside Sicily, his favourite kingdom, and even Sicily in his day included the southern part of the Italian mainland.

As grandson of the great Emperor Barbarossa and Roger II of Sicily, his legitimacy was naturally of supreme importance, which is why Constance, then aged forty-two, deemed it prudent to be confined in a tent in the market place of Jesi, where any matron who wished could be an eye-witness of the event. No one could then deny that he was the legitimate descendant of the Norman kings, but attempts to throw doubt on his paternity were inevitable, in view of the probability that this infant would one day inherit Germany and a great part of Italy. Constance's lack of prudery forestalled the later rumour that Frederick was really the substituted son of the town butcher and persuaded the world that he was the son of a far greater one; even so, in an age of superstition, when prophets were busy foretelling the arrival of a Saviour, a Scourge of the World or an Antichrist, according to taste, Abbot Joachim from Calabria hinted to the expectant father that his wife had been made pregnant by one of those demons, recognized in mediaeval law, who practised the exotic speciality of having carnal knowledge of sleeping women.

Frederick's father died when the child was only three, and Constance survived him for a short time only. The child was left a ward of the Pope and grew up far from intrigues in the royal park of Palermo. The city's oriental atmosphere and the licence which permitted him to run wild among Moslems, Jews and Italians, enabled him to mix with all classes—a trait inherited from his grandfather Barbarossa—and learn some of the nine languages he was later reputed to speak. It was during these years that he grew to love wild life and venery, for both kinds of which he later became so justly famed.

Physically, he grew to middle height, broadly proportioned, agile and skilled in horsemanship and the use of arms. His red-gold hair and blue eyes could be traced either to his Viking ancestors—his mother was a typical Nordic woman—or to his paternal grandfather, Frederick Barbarossa, him of the red beard. Historians describe him as handsome and of kingly bearing, even in his youth, for his precocity astonished even the Pope and the latter thought nothing of marrying him to Constance, the twenty-four-year-old widow of the King of Hungary, when Frederick was fourteen. Special mention is made of his level gaze and one Arab historian even said that he squinted, but the squint, it should be remembered, was regarded as the sign of a proud spirit. Possibly this was the origin of the legend of his short-sightedness; I say legend, for it was manifestly impossible for anyone to follow the sport of falconry, let alone to write a book about it, if he was near-sighted before the days of concave spectacle lenses.

His titles need not concern us, but they must have contributed to his conviction that he was the incarnation of a Roman emperor, I mean a real one and not just a Holy imitation, like his father and grandfather. When he was four he was crowned King of Sicily and greeted, as was customary, with the words: *Christus vincit, Christus regnat, Christus imperat*, words which are still found on the crucifixes of southern Italy. It cannot have been too great a step to the concept of himself as Christ's regent, conqueror, ruler, emperor. His coins, some of the most impressive ever minted, showed his profile with laurel weath in classical style, with the legend, which I need not translate, IMP. ROM. CESAR AUG. and the Roman eagle on the reverse. When we passed through the little Sicilian port of Augusta during the last war we could see one of Frederick's castles above the town that he founded and named with typical imperial ostentation; now it looks down on one of the main ports for refining and exporting mineral oil, whose recent discovery threatens to change Sicily's picturesque squalor into squalid affluence.

Frederick's marriages were purely political but he is alleged, nevertheless, to have kept his wives fairly contented, a gift which many an adulterer must envy. When Number Two, Yolande de Brienne, aged fourteen, arrived at Brindisi, the wedding and Frederick's resulting claim to the throne of Jerusalem were signalized with the greatest pomp; possibly to compensate himself for the tedious ceremony he spent the night with Yolande's pretty and maturer cousin, rightly assuming that the bride could wait for a night or two. Of all his wives, mistresses, casual acquaintances and Moslem dancing (or sewing) girls, his one love seems to have been Bianca Lancia, sister of Frederick's great friend Manfred. Bianca's son was also called Manfred, and through him the succession eventually passed to Spain, as will be related. Though the name Lancia is a common one in Italy, both for men and motor cars, authentic descendants of Frederick and Bianca's daughter survived for centuries; in the cemetery of Santo Spirito, the so-called Church of the Vespers in Palermo, you may today see the tomb of a Lancia who could trace his descent in an unbroken line, and was buried in 1883.

As a ruler, Frederick was far in advance of his time and the Constitutions of Melfi, with their concern for pauper, widow and orphan, seem quite out of place in the world he lived in. Only in his dealings with the Moslems of Sicily do we detect the results of misrule, for their rebellion seems to have stemmed to a large extent from repressive measures which Frederick introduced with a view to conciliating the Pope. The campaign, or rather series of campaigns, took several years, and the question was solved only by transporting large numbers of Sicilian Moslems to Lucera, a new settlement on the mainland built to Moslem specifications, with mosques, minarets, muezzins, caids and everything else that could make a Sicilian Mohamedan feel at home. It is pleasant to read that the Saracens of Lucera provided some of the bravest and most loyal of his and his successor's guards. They also took with them their own arts and crafts, so that on the fall of Lucera fifty years later, the conquering Angevin made provision for the transport to Naples of various specialists, among whom the cushion embroiderers were singled out for mention.

Frederick's efforts at conciliating the Popes did not prevent an almost constant hostility, with two excommunications; his liberal views and scientific mind could not but antagonize "the Establishment"; his tardiness in undertaking the promised crusade provided a convenient reason, but the inevitability of the struggle was obvious and stemmed from the fact that the Guelph party supported the Popes, while Frederick was a Ghibelline. So much was this so that the green of the Ghibelline faction was adopted from Frederick's favourite wear, the huntsman's tunic. What made him more hated than any other single action was that he eventually conducted the crusade for whose postponement he had been excommunicated, and recovered the holy places for which so much blood had been shed over so many years, by simple statesmanlike negotiation with the Arab emir, whose language he of course spoke fluently. But all this has little to do with Sicily, as indeed has the subject of his hobbies; they are too interesting, however, to be entirely omitted.

When Matthew Paris referred to the "marvellous innovator" he was probably not thinking of an invention which caused more talk than any other at the time: whereas his predecessors had been content to keep an oriental harem of dancing (or sewing) girls at home in Sicily, with the regulation eunuch guards, Frederick, profiting from the lessons he had learned during his crusade, introduced the travelling harem, so convenient for a monarch whose wide possessions extended from the North Sea to the Mediterranean. His private zoo travelled with him too, and the three leopards he sent to the King of England, in allusion to the royal coat of arms, were the founder members of the menagerie at the Tower of London. He was more than a collector, though; he was a scientist. Doubting the accepted belief that certain geese were hatched from barnacles, he had a pair of barnacle geese brought to him from Iceland and demonstrated how they reproduced in the normal way. How hard these fallacies die! A special kind of barnacle, called *percebe*, is a delicacy among preprandial snacks in Spain; on looking up the word in a dictionary, you will find it rendered "goose barnacle". And, as a matter of fact, if you compare *percebes* with the feet of barnacle geese (there are some in Saint James's Park in London) you will find an extraordinary resemblance. Among his other achievements in nature study was the observation that a nestling differed from its fellows; using what are now accepted methods of scientific inquiry, he propounded and then proved the theory of the nesting habits of the cuckoo. He was probably the first man for fifteen centuries to question any dictum of Aristotle and, where he doubted him, to put the matter to the test. That was the sort of behaviour that made men unpopular in the Middle Ages, and often does today, for that matter.

Though Palermo was a link with Byzantium at this time, and a clearing house for much imported oriental wisdom, it is a fallacy to suppose that Frederick spent much time there, in spite of the legends that grew up about his brilliant Palermitan court. This is possibly due to the wide fame of his "Sicilian Questions", five philosophical puzzles which he caused to circulate throughout the Arab world; they were hardly what one would expect from a Christian, but could proceed quite suitably from one who had been excommunicated for the second time. The question which brings us nearest to his mind is the fifth: "How are the words of Mohamed explained—'The heart of the believer is between the two fingers of the Merciful'?". The replies of Ibn Sab'in are preserved, and in them too we sense the struggle between a free spirit and the restraints of orthodoxy. Question and answer reached Pope Innocent IV quite soon—communications in those days were better than we believe—and no doubt confirmed him in his abhorrence of the heretic emperor.

Another surprise awaits those who have been taught that all was darkness before the Renaissance. Had Frederick lived longer, or the Popes been less obscurantist, the links which existed between east and west might have introduced the new humanism two hundred years earlier. An earlier Columbus might have sailed before 1300, a Napoleon have met his Waterloo in 1615 and we might have been annihilated by hydrogen bombs long before this book was written. Mathematics had already made great strides, partly from the dissemination of Indian and Iranian wisdom, and it was at a scientific tournament sponsored by Frederick that the famous Leonardo Fibonacci of Pisa was presented to the emperor and demonstrated his brilliancy in solving algebraic problems which would be considered too difficult for a University entrance examination today. But the earlier Renaissance was not destined to flourish, for, as Cajori says: "During the fourteenth and fifteenth centuries, the mathematical science was almost stationary. Long wars absorbed the energies of the people and thereby kept back the growth of the sciences. The death of Frederick II in 1254* was followed by a period of confusion in Germany. The German emperors and the Popes were continually quarrelling, and Italy was inevitably drawn into the struggles between the Guelphs and Ghibellines. France and England were engaged in the Hundred Years' War." Cajori might have added that the flow of knowledge from the east had been interrupted by the appalling devastations of Genghis Khan, one of Frederick's better known contemporaries. Another was Saint Francis of Assisi, returning from his solitary visit—almost a one-man crusade—to the Sultan Al-Kamil, the same with whom Frederick later made his famous treaty for the Holy sites. The legend that the Emperor caused a seductive temptress to be introduced into the Saint's room and then watched proceedings through the keyhole could, if true, be ascribed to his scientific curiosity.

Among Frederick's loyal supporters, and there were few who stood by him in adversity, was Hermann von Salza, Grand Master of the Teutonic Order; like the Order of Saint John it had begun as a nursing service for pilgrims and later became militant. When Frederick crowned himself in the Church of the Holy Sepulchre in Jerusalem, his faithful Teutonic Knights provided a large part of the congregation, and years before that they had been charged with the task of converting the Prussian heathen, an assignment which they completed with apparent success; no stigma attached to the fact that the recently converted were simultaneously transformed into serfs and that the knights acquired those large estates which, in our own time, were the property of the powerful and reactionary Baltic barons. In Palermo the Order was given one of the Cistercian churches as its headquarters, whence it took the usual name of *mansio*, or mansion, now corrupted to La Magione. Rebuilt since its destruction in the late war, it still preserves three of the tombs of its occupants, transferred from the body of the church to the cloister. To visit La Magione you have to traverse a part of Palermo infested by hooligans and pickpockets and one can only wish that the dead knights would arise from their graves, like the grenadier in Heine's poem, and protect one.

The Cistercians were greatly favoured by the emperor and from them came the Suevic or Swabian style, which can best be described as a grafting

* The correct date is 13th December, 1250.—A. L.

94

of Gothic on Sicilian Norman architecture and decoration; later, the same style included ideas which Frederick brought back from his crusade, best seen in his secular buildings, which incorporate oriental features that cannot be attributed to the Sicilian saracens. The castles at Augusta and Syracuse are the best examples in the island, but the often quoted Castel del Monte in Apulia is a still more instructive specimen. Modica's Church of Santa Maria di Betlem keeps more than its Suevic architecture, for it has retained the Cistercian custom of ringing the noon bell at 11 a.m., when Cistercians traditionally eat their principal meal.

Frederick's love of falconry and his mastery of the subject have been preserved for all time in his manual, *De arte venandi cum avibus* (On the art of hunting with birds), which he wrote for his son Manfred. It throws so much light on Frederick as a true sportsman and nature lover that one can gain an insight into at least one facet of his complex character, and that perhaps the most attractive. Those who are interested may consult an English translation or, if they want the essentials only, read the masterly section in Georgina Masson's book. I sometimes wonder whether our word "saker" for a cannon owes its origin to Frederick, for the original Arabic *saqr* is a species of falcon and the word came to Europe with the same meaning. When firearms were invented they were sometimes named after animals, for instance "culverin" and "dragoon" from real and mythical serpents, but especially from birds of prey, whence falconet, musket and, of course, saker.

10 *The Sicilian Vespers and After*

Frederick's death removed the strongest opposition to papal aspirations. It was therefore inevitable that the Hohenstaufen line would be extinguished; Conrad died in 1254 and Manfred, inheriting much of his father's ability, was for a time the factual ruler of Italy. Two French Popes, however, succeeded in eliminating him, Urban IV by inviting Charles of Anjou to claim the Sicilian crown, and Clement IV by supporting his campaign. Charles, the heavy jawed, long-nosed younger brother of Saint Louis, King of France, shows up badly in the light of history; admittedly it must have been a strain living up to the saintly example of his brother, who not only embarked on two crusades with maximum piety and inefficiency but also disapproved of papal intolerance of Frederick, thus teaching the Pope a lesson in Christianity. This pious bungler sternly rejected the papal invitation to assume the crown of Sicily, and his brother Charles is said to have done so only to oblige his wife. For the Countess Beatrice, watching a festival procession, was forced to leave the dais on which her younger sisters, Queens of France and England, were sitting; quite naturally, she returned to her room in tears, where Charles found her and, kissing her lips, said "Countess, set your mind at ease, for I will soon make you a greater queen than they." The bargain was promptly struck; Beatrice pawned her jewels to supply a part of the funds, Clement IV produced the rest, as well as the necessary blessing of the Church, in exchange for much territory between Naples and Benevento. Helped by treachery—Dante has something to say about this—Charles crossed the Garigliano and then, helped by luck, won the battle of Benevento, where Manfred met his death. Two years later Conradin, the sixteen-year-old grandson of Frederick II, invaded Italy over the Alps, while some of his supporters landed in Sciacca. Fortune was again on the side of Charles, whose troops defeated Conradin at the battle of Tagliacozzo. The unfortunate lad fled and, seeking refuge with Giovanni Frangipane, was sold by his host to Charles of Anjou. Quite the most ruthless of the characters we have so far encountered, Charles had Conradin condemned by a so-called court of justice and beheaded in the market place of Naples, an unheard of fate for a captured claimant to a throne.

It was believed that, after the execution, Charles of Anjou, in the words of Amari, "in observance of a semi-pagan superstition derived from Greece, had caused a soup to be made, which he had eaten upon the corpses of Conradin and his fellow-sufferers; this rite was supposed to cleanse the

I (a) *ERICE—Church, Monte Cofano*

(b) *SEGESTA—Temple*

II (a) *SALEMI—Breath-taking hill town*

(b) *MOTYA—Along the water's edge*

III *ERICE—Cathedral with square belfry tower*

IV (a) *ERICE—Norman Castello*

(b) *CAMPOBELLO—Boulder from Cusa quarry*

V (a) *S. CROCE DI CAMERINA—The Cuba*

(b) *PIAZZA ARMERINA—Mosaics*

VI *S. TRINITA DI DELIA—Near Castelvetrano*

VII   (a) *TAORMINA—Macri's puppets from Acireale*

(b) *PALERMO—La Martorana; George of Antioch and Roger II*

VIII (a) *PALERMO—S. Giovanni degli Erimiti*
(b) *CEFALU—Mother and daughter washing clothes*

observer from the guilt of homicide". Dante, in his *Purgatory*,* obviously believed the story and disapproved of the action. Primitive tribes practise various magical ceremonies, from drinking medicines to smearing themselves with goat's dung, to keep away the spirit of their victim. We may sense the same magic when Abu al-'Abbas had all but one of the rival Omayyads massacred while seated peacefully in his palace. When the last victim had been clubbed to death the Abbassid ordered a carpet to be spread over the corpses, and ate a meal on it.

The other story relates how the young Conradin, a moment before his execution, looked down from the scaffold and, tossing a glove into the crowd, said "This for Peter." Now Conradin was the last legitimate male descendant of Frederick, and with him perished the Hohenstaufen line, but his cousin Constance had married Peter of Aragón; we shall learn how Peter, at least figuratively, picked up the gage.

A glimpse of the character of Charles of Anjou can be obtained from the story of the eighth, or last crusade. Louis IX, saint and king, had thought to recapture the Holy City by attacking Egypt. Landing at Damietta, he contrived, by means of bad staff work, worse logistics and incredible strategy, to lose his army, his liberty, a ransom of half a million gold pounds, and his health. Joinville gives an excellent description of the scurvy from which the Christian host was suffering, and of the dysentery (probably another manifestation of malnutrition) which accompanied it and became the king's sorest trial. "That night he fainted several times," he wrote, "and because of the sore dysentery from which he suffered, it was necessary to cut away the lower part of his drawers, so frequent were his necessities."

Charles of Anjou, who had accompanied the ill-fated crusade of 1248–9, and distinguished himself in this débâcle, encouraged his old and ailing brother to attempt a last crusade in Tunis, so near to the newly acquired kingdom of Sicily, by spreading a rumour to the effect that the Bey wished to be converted to Christianity. As usual, poor Louis blundered into a trap; his army was blockaded in Carthage, where the wells had been deliberately poisoned, he, his son Tristam and many of his nobles perished and the crusade collapsed. At this juncture, Charles of Anjou, who had been waiting in nearby Sicily, sailed across the strait and made a treaty with the Saracens, guaranteeing the immunity of Sicily in return for the departure of the crusaders; in addition he accepted a fairly large sum of money and an increase of the annual tribute which the Bey of Tunis had formerly paid to King Roger II and his successors.

Disgusted with Charles's perfidy, Prince Edward of England set sail for Acre on an abortive private crusade; there, as we all learned in our history books, he was stabbed with a poisoned dagger, saved by his noble wife—she can hardly have known that venoms used in this way are harmless when

* "... *Ma chi n'ha colpa creda,*
Che vendetta di Dio non teme suppe."

97

taken by mouth—and returned to England, where he found that his father had died and that his new duties as King Edward I kept him fully occupied. Had he stayed with his fellow-crusaders in Tunis he would have witnessed something which would really have turned his stomach. When the ships, laden with gold and returning crusaders, anchored in Trapani, "divine vengeance", in the shape of a storm, sank the fleet and all the treasure; but it would take more than that to baffle Charles of Anjou, who made a profit out of his companions' misfortunes by invoking an old statute which empowered him to appropriate the goods of shipwrecked persons. The later story, that Charles himself sank the crusading fleet, is too good to be true.

Twelve years later, French rule, or misrule, in Sicily came to an end. Seething with the discontent that followed the rapacity of their new rulers, the debasement of their coinage and the arrogance of the French garrisons, the islanders rose in furious revolt. The trivial incident which triggered off the explosion occurred in Palermo on Easter Monday,* 31st March, 1282. At the hour of the vespers a bridal couple were entering the Church of Santo Spirito; a French sergeant, named Drouet, stopped them and, under the humorous pretext of examining her for concealed weapons, put his hand down the girl's dress. Within minutes he, and every other French soldier in the vicinity was dead. The church bells rang furiously as the revolution spread through the island, and when the French severed the bell-ropes the Sicilians used hammers, a custom that survived during Lent into the present century. Mounted messengers carried the news with all the speed they could, and the massacre spread to every town in the island but one; at Sperlinga the French were so well liked that the townsfolk refused to attack them. The Castle of Sperlinga still raises its ruined towers amid the swirling clouds, notable for the fact that large parts of it are hollowed out of the solid rock, in whose faces are cut the gutters which brought drinking water to the garrison. You approach the outer gate up a steep path paved with goat droppings; inside, a short passage leads you to the well-preserved inner gate, on whose arch is inscribed the famous motto: "*Quod Siculis placuit sola Sperlinga negavit*—What the Sicilians wanted, only Sperlinga refused." The aptness of the verse partly atones for the false quantity in *sola*, which would no doubt have earned the composer, if a schoolboy, a stay in the castle dungeons on bread and water.

Sperlinga must have represented a strange oasis of peace amidst the universal massacre, in which not only the French, but any Sicilian female unfortunate enough to be pregnant by a Frenchman, were slaughtered and, in appropriate cases, ripped up so that even the French embryo could be destroyed. But in Sperlinga all was peace, and even today the inhabitants speak a debased French dialect; in any part of Sicily one may come across linguistic oddities, Lombard dialects that would sound more natural in the

* Tuesday is often mentioned, but the chronicles are quite explicit in naming the second day of Easter.

Po valley, words like *boatta* for box, which obviously comes from the French *boîte*, and relics of the centuries of Spanish domination. Many a French friar lost his life at the hands of the angry mob, who adopted a variant of the test made famous by the men of Gilead, but instead of asking suspects to say "Shibboleth" they chose the word *"ciciri"*, which no Frenchman could pronounce aright.

Of course there was more to the Vespers than a spontaneous rising against the hand of France in the bosom of Sicily. Charles of Anjou was preparing an expeditionary force to attempt the conquest of Constantinople, a favourite diversion of pseudo-crusaders, who hoped for more loot and less fighting in that city than in Saracen territory. The emperor Michael Palaeologus, making money do the work of men, financed John of Procida, a physician who had attended Frederick II in his last illness, to sow the seeds of revolt and at the same time interest Peter, King of Aragón, in a possible conquest. Verdi's opera, *I Vespri Siciliani*, was composed to the libretto of the French playwright Scribe (the American Express in Paris is right up his street) and therefore makes a villain out of John of Procida; one is still uncertain of the part he played, but it is unlikely that Charles of Anjou had made an enemy of him by seducing his wife Pandolfina. The result was at all events highly satisfactory to all except Charles: the Angevin fleet was burned at Messina before it could sail for the conquest of Constantinople; Peter of Aragón was "persuaded" to abandon a faked crusade which he was conducting at Collo near Tunis, very handy for Sicily; and the War of the Vespers was largely conducted at sea and in France and Spain.

The war itself lasted twenty years and simply confirmed the King of Aragón as ruler of Sicily. It provided the first battleground for the *almogavares*, Catalan highlanders who considered themselves more than a match for any French soldier, however well armed. These ragamuffins, deprived of fighting and plunder once the French were expelled, joined up with the notorious Roger de Flor; Roger was really the son of Frederick II's Chief Falconer, named Von Blum, and the change of name was a literal one. Such a leader, with such men, was bound to leave his mark, and it is as well for Sicily that their activities were channelled into the Eastern Empire. The Catalan navy was also a formidable one and far superior to the Provençal fleet of Charles. In the great sea fight of 1283 the Catalans completely routed a greater number of the enemy by the use of such unsporting tricks as throwing fireballs into their ships, lime in their eyes and soap and tallow on to the rowers' benches, so that the unfortunate oarsmen slipped about and never got the necessary purchase to get their galleys moving.

Both Charles of Anjou and Peter of Aragón died before the end of the War of the Vespers, but the former's attempt to reconquer the island from Messina, after landing at Milazzo, failed dismally. Peace was finally signed at Caltabellotta in 1302 and the island settled down to over four centuries of Spanish rule, consoling itself with the reflection that it might have been worse, for Sicilians have always resented a government based on Naples.

Little interest or importance attaches to the period of Spanish domination. The royal house of Aragón provided rulers, first in the person of relatives, later of viceroys. It was at this time that the French family of Clermont came to prominence; their name, altered to Chiaramonte, was applied to a style of architecture, of which a charming piece survives at Modica in the home of the De Leva family, of Spanish descent as their name

shows. Originally the entrance to a chapel, it now gives access to a store room and adds a delightful touch to the front of Sr. Pietro de Leva's town house. Here one can see quite plainly [*opposite*] how the leaf patterns modify the severity of the Norman and Gothic elements of the portal, as in the Convent of Santo Spirito in Agrigento [*below*]. A similar lightness of decoration can be seen in the triple windows which relieve the stern façade of Lo Steri in Palermo. If you are in Modica and have time to see this gem of Chiaramontine style in the De Leva house, you may be lucky enough to meet the owner and receive that blend of Spanish courtesy and Sicilian hospitality which is so characteristic of the island. You may also see the earliest Spanish influence on mediaeval styles in the Church of Carmine.

It is customary to describe the centuries of Spanish rule as a time of unrelieved degradation. This, I suggest, requires a new assessment: during the 400 years that saw large tracts of France devastated by the English and then by her own religious wars, Ireland ruined by Cromwell, the Low Countries savagely suppressed by Spain, Italy marauded by bands of military parasites, papal and profane, and eastern Europe as far as the Adriatic and Vienna in Turkish hands, Sicily enjoyed her privations in peace. True, she contributed handsomely to the fleet, commanded by Don John of Austria, that won the battle of Lepanto and kept the Turks from the western Mediterranean; a smaller force was included in the Spanish Armada and, far more important, more Sicilian timber was hewn down and more soil erosion caused.

The decline of Sicily is often blamed on Spanish misrule. This is true, but only in so far as Spain herself declined at the same speed. In the heyday of Spanish power, under the Holy Roman Emperor Charles V, Sicily obtained her share of improvements and suffered the depredations of the improvers. Parts of the Greek theatre at Syracuse were used to construct defensive

walls and the mole at Porta Empedocle was built from blocks of the temple of Heracles at Agrigento. Such destruction would cause no comment in the sixteenth century.

Spain's rule over Sicily ceased with the War of the Spanish Succession at the beginning of the eighteenth century. From then on she became a pawn in power politics, eventually coming under the rule of the kingdom of Naples. Her role in the Napoleonic wars was a dramatic one. Across the stage flitted the figures of King Ferdinand, whom Herold describes as "a man with the countenance (and mentality) of a prosperous village idiot"; of his wife, obsessed with the fate of her sister Marie Antoinette; of Emma Hamilton and the colourful and controversial Nelson; and of Sir William Bentinck, who gave the country its first parliamentary government. After his recall, however, the country relapsed into a Bourbon appendage, with all the accompaniment of police spies, midnight shootings and mysterious disappearances. Revolt after revolt broke out and was crushed, and patriots like Amari, Stabile and Settimo achieved momentary success and immortal fame, until Garibaldi and his Thousand once and for all removed the Bourbon pest.

Much has happened in Sicily since then: the greatest of all wars has passed through, autonomy has been obtained and mineral wealth discovered. These things will be history one day; they have little relevance now for the visitor who comes to enjoy Sicily's historic legacies. But he may remember the fateful days of 1942 and 1943, and how Sicily changed from barrier to bridge overnight.

PART II—MAINLY PLACES

11 *Palermo—The Main Artery*

The chances are that this, the capital of Sicily, will also be your point of arrival by air, sea or rail. The motorist who takes the long, leisurely drive through Calabria will of course arrive in Messina; but so terribly was this city damaged in the earthquake of 1908 that there remain but few historical reminders. Palermo, on the other hand, is redolent of the past and manages to combine the modern activities of a large city with an atmosphere that takes you back one or two or more centuries. Strangely, though, its tangible relics extend only, or almost only, to the Norman period. There was a Phoenician town here, and a Greek one on the same site, and a Roman one thereafter, but for the visitor they might as well have never existed. Their site was on the hill where the cathedral and the Norman palace now stand; it is approached along the Corso Vittorio Emanuele, which runs west from the sea front. This is the Cassaro Vecchio which has from time immemorial connected the raised strong point with the harbour; the latter has receded over the years and reached its present position at about the middle of the sixteenth century. The small basin for fishing boats, called the *Cala*, is all that is left of this inlet.

The word Cassaro is the Arabic *Kasr* (as in the Alcázar of Granada) which in turn comes from the Latin *castrum*, and the Cassaro Vecchio takes you, as its name implies, to the old fort which the Normans converted into their royal palace. If you find the seaward end at the Porta Felice, reconstructed since the unnecessarily thorough bombardment of the port area in 1943, you will be very near to the Church of Santa Maria della Catena, a fine mixture of Renaissance and Gothic styles, with a touch of Catalan. The loggia, reached by the spacious steps, would not be out of place in Florence and the complicated vaulting ribs remind one of many a Spanish church interior. The name, however, is more interesting than the church; Saint Mary of the Chain is situated only a hundred yards from the old *dogana* or custom house, now the Chiaramonte Palace, and the harbour could be closed at this point by means of a chain stretched across, presumably to avoid by-passing the revenue officials. This undoubtedly goes back to

Norman times, for they used the Arabic *diwan* in the sense of a council and hence the fiscal department, which apparently derived most of its revenue from customs duties, was known as the *diwan*, or *dohana de secretis* which in turn gave us *dogana, aduana* and *douane*, in the various tongues of modern Europe.

Though this quarter, still called Kalsa from the Arabic *khalis*, pure, seems to beckon us with every corner, we must resolutely postpone our visit and set out for the magnificent sights at the west end of the Corso. The part that we are on, by the way, is called the Cassaro Morto, only too aptly since the last war. Going westward, between buildings which, in the main, represent some of the best Renaissance and Baroque façades, we cross the Via Roma and note that the harbour originally extended to this point. The next crossing is the well-known Quattro Canti, or Four Corners, which marks the crossing of the Cassaro Nuovo, as our street is now called, and the Via Maqueda, named after one of the Spanish viceroys. Away on our right is the new town; before we reach it there are several points of interest, including the Archaeological Museum; beyond that the only history note that I detected was a plaque on the wall of a house, stating that the hotel where Wagner lived was in that building, situated at the corner of Via Mariano Stabile and, of course, the Via Riccardo Wagner. I have the greatest difficulty in relating the ponderous, Teutonic strains of *Parsifal* with the tropical garden of the Palazzo Rufolo in Ravello, where Wagner found the inspiration for his magic garden of Klingsor, and semi-oriental Palermo, where he completed the work.

The Quattro Canti is not to everyone's taste, but it still serves the purpose for which it was built, to mark the centre of the old city. Each corner has a Spanish king of Sicily, one of the Seasons and one of the city's patron saints (or, as they are all females—Agata, Cristina, Ninfa and Oliva—should it be "patroness saints", or even "matron saints"? There is an obvious deficiency in our language here.) Each corner also bears an inscribed plaque, drawing attention to the generosity of viceroys, all with Spanish names and titles.

A few yards to the left, along the Via Maqueda, a low flight of steps takes you to the Piazza Pretoria, among whose crowded parked cars rises the sixteenth century Florentine fountain, whose huge marble basin and gleaming pseudo-classical, pseudo-modest statues make a fine show against the old buildings that form the square. I have purposely brought you here at this point in our stroll, for the exuberance of the fountain would probably irritate you after the wonders we are about to see. An amusing feature, literally, is provided by the noses of some of the male statues: these, if you look carefully, can be seen to have been broken off and replaced and are today about the only reminder of centuries of rivalry between Palermo and Messina. It seems that certain men of Messina, one night in the distant past, carried the vendetta a step further by breaking off those noses. Not, you would think, a particularly offensive piece of strategy unless you know two facts; first, that the ancient Sicilian punishment for panders was to cut off their noses, and secondly, that even today the rudest gesture you can make to a Sicilian, equivalent to calling him a *ruffiano*, or pimp, is to take your nose between finger and thumb and give it a twist.

Leaving the Piazza Pretoria through the south-eastern corner you will be inclined to rub your eyes. Opposite, across a narrow piazza, stand two churches, that on the left noteworthy for its campanile, fortunately spared during the barbarous alterations of the seventeenth century [*below*]. Note the twin windows and the "billet" frame on the first floor, both features commonly and incorrectly attributed to Arab invention, as was the case with the chevron. The "billets", for instance, can be seen in Oxfordshire, on the Church of Saint Mary at Iffley. The other two storeys of this enchanting tower do, however, show a genuinely oriental peculiarity, the engaged column at each angle. Seen from where you are standing and rising out of a bed of tropical foliage, it balances the massive four-square bulk of the other church, surprisingly crowned with three cupolas, exactly like those of S. Trinità di Delia [*Col. pl. VI*] except for their faded tomato colour. It is the colour more than anything else which persuades you that what you are look-

ing at can never be matched outside this island, where two civilizations lived harmoniously together, each borrowing and lending what either needed. There are many greater and more gorgeous buildings, from India to Spain, but none that evoke quite the same emotion as do these hybrids of Sicily.

The church on the left is called S. Maria del Ammiraglio, after the founder, George of Antioch, admiral and general combined, who conquered Tunis, Corfu and Cephalonia and ravaged much of western Greece in the years 1146–8. Some time before this he had founded the church, now usually called La Martorana from the fortuitous circumstance that it was presented in 1433 to a convent founded in 1194 by Eloisa Martorana; a few columns from the cloister still survive. There is a bit of a mystery about the campanile, which resembles those of the cathedral very closely. According to Bottari, our leading authority, the change from the plain surfaces constructed by the Arabs to the high relief that we see here, with its contrasting light and shade, occurred just at the moment when the Norman kingdom of Tancred collapsed and Arab master-builders were forced to leave Sicily in the early days of the Suevic dynasty. This would put the completion of the campanile in the last decade of the twelfth century; the influence of Western European Romanesque at this stage can be seen with ease by comparing La Martorana with S. Trinità di Delia.

The interior is also of great interest, once you have determined precisely where the Baroque vandals stopped their "improvements" and allowed the Byzantine mosaics to remain on the upper walls and cupola. Near the entrance, on one side, is a mosaic of George of Antioch grovelling at the feet of the Virgin, in a style characteristically Byzantine, which in this case means oriental [*Col. pl. VII(b and c)*]; fittingly enough it had been introduced to the western world before A.D. 300 by Diocletian, to whom may in a sense be attributed the founding of an Eastern Roman Empire. The original from which this may be taken is a mosaic of about A.D. 900 in Istanbul's Hagia Sophia, where Leo VI is seen kneeling in the same supplicating posture, at the feet of Christ. On the other side Roger II, suitably diminished in size (a pictorial convention that goes back to the Pharaohs), receives a crown from the Saviour. An interesting glimpse of the Norman court can be obtained from the fact that the words *Rogerios Rex*, themselves in a kind of Hellenized Latin, are produced with Greek lettering. Note also that the king is wearing the girdle, stole and maniple of a bishop, a privilege specially granted to Sicilian monarchs by the Pope. My favourite ceiling mosaic is the Nativity in which the artist, determined to leave out nothing, has included the star with a single ray falling on the swaddled infant, who lies on an altar rather than in a crib, an early example of the western concept of the sacrificial victim. The ox and the ass, of course, are peeping at Him, in accordance with the Isaiah text, angels fill up empty spaces and one of them blesses, in eastern style, the shepherds with their rudimentary sheep and one goat. A worried Saint Joseph takes the bottom left corner, and opposite him another episode, in the manner that survives in the comic strip, shows the midwives preparing to bath another Infant Jesus, presumably after the episode of the withered hand restored, which figures in the apocryphal Gospel of Pseudo-Matthew. The story of the midwives, Salome and Zelemie, had a short life and died out in the middle of the thirteenth century, presumably because Saint Jerome had denied that midwives were present and had maintained that the Virgin herself had swaddled the Infant, so that "*ipsa et mater et obstetrix fuit*". Before leaving the church note that the geometrical Arab style of decoration is uncommon in Sicily, and a twelfth century carved wooden door on your left provides a good example.

Built on the same plinth, a few yards away, is the slightly later and obviously restored Church of San Cataldo, which we distinguished earlier by its red cupolas. The interiors of these will interest the architect, with the receding orders of arch in each squinch, a form which I believe comes originally from Persia. The column capitals, too, are interesting, five of them being classical Corinthian and the sixth, presumably Byzantine, of a very queer pattern indeed. The floor is of really old *opus alexandrinum* and the cool, restful, atmosphere is an aid to meditation and an antidote to travel fatigue.

Returning to the Corso and continuing westward, we are soon treading the site of the original town, an oval enclosed between two rivers, the Papireto on your right and the Maltempo on your left, both now piped away from their swampy beds. The area of the Papireto was one of the Moslem quarters after the Norman conquest, and persecution of the Moslems in later days usually began with these unfortunates. It is fairly certain that the name commemorates a plantation of papyrus, possibly grown with a view to providing writing material, the same which Benjamin of Tudela described.

Very soon an open space appears on your right, surrounded by late Baroque balustrades and statues, and there, its vast southern wall relieved by an occasional palm tree, is the Norman cathedral [*below*]. Its massive and intricate campanile, at the west end, needs two great arches that span

the street to join it to the main building; at each corner smaller towers, one with a clock, recall the campanile of La Martorana [below]. One cannot but admire this great, tawny mass, even though the purist pretends to shudder at the mixture of styles. Pointed Saracenic windows and blind arcades, rounded Norman merlons and a horrible eighteenth-century dome compete for recognition and just manage to avoid a fight. The main entrance is also on this southern side, a graceful Gothic porch with three arches. The left pillar bears an Arabic inscription and is usually said to have belonged to the mosque that once stood on this site; though no support is adduced for this belief, reading the text shows that it is a quotation from the *Koran*, verse 55

of Sura VII to be exact, beginning "Our Lord God created the day followed by the night", and this of course strengthens the claim. The purest Siculo-Norman feature is the eastern elevation, where the apses are decorated with interlacing arches and medallions, and with abstract patterns designed with blocks of black lava. It has been suggested that the pointed Saracenic arch actually originated from the pattern made by the interlacing of less pointed, or even semicircular arches, as in the case of S. Spirito [below].

As you enter through the porch you pass under a small Byzantine Madonna in mosaic and through the handsome fifteenth-century portal and carved doors. The interior is disappointing, for Fuga, who built the hideous dome (though it might have passed unnoticed anywhere else) completely ruined the interior with baroque decoration. There is much to see, nevertheless. The tombs of Norman and Hohenstaufen royalties have been described and pictured often enough; the shape of the porphyry sarcophagi and the lions which support that of Frederick II, "*Stupor Mundi*", became fashionable throughout Sicily. Very often a vase of flowers, garden picked and humble, stands on the floor before this tomb, but I have never discovered who brings this tribute to Caesar's mouldering bones. His first wife,

Constance of Aragón, occupies an antique sarcophagus set in the wall on the right; her crown, which was found intact when the tomb was opened during the last century, will interest us when we reach the treasury. His parents rest in two of the other porphyry sarcophagi, which Frederick had brought from Cefalù, having first sent the Bishop on an embassy to Syria so that the coast might be clear for what was virtually a theft. From this, and much other evidence, Bottari concludes that Frederick's sarcophagus was made after his death, on the initiative of his son and successor Manfred. The statement by Kantorowicz, the emperor's great biographer, that the supporting lions are engraved with prehistoric South Italian symbols, would take some explaining if Bottari is right. I therefore made a diligent search for these symbols; there are none. The columns supporting the canopies of most of these tombs have mosaic lozenges and chevrons, typical of the Cosmati school and once more not attributable to Sicilian Moslem influences. At the far end of the nave is an impressive Paschal candle-holder, mis-called "Moorish" for the same reason. On the floor, before reaching the choir, is a strip adorned with the signs of the zodiac and a hole in the roof allows a ray of sunshine to enter at noon and thus lets one read the approximate date. The sextant uses the same principle of course, but for the purpose of determining latitude. A true sundial, constructed on a similar principle and giving the time of day, may be seen in the Church of S. Pietro in Castiglione (see Chapter VI).

The treasury has many interesting exhibits, but the so-called crown of Constance, more probably a jewelled cap of maintenance, is its star exhibit. I have been fortunate enough to be allowed to examine it closely, with the glass front of the show-case opened, and can vouch for the wonderful preservation of the textile and even the stitching. The jewels, as is usual in mediaeval finery, are unimpressive, but certainly contribute to the regal appearance of the cap. The sacristan will point out a ruby in the front, on which some Arabic is engraved; when asked what the engraving says, he confesses that he has no idea. This is not surprising, for the writing is mirror fashion, with points and vowel signs omitted, and the jewel was obviously a seal stone, probably from a Saracen's ring; the nearest I could get to reading the lettering was "*Khalis ibn-Hawas*", which sounds suspiciously like one of the emirs of central Sicily who fought against Count Roger. The ruby, by the way, is a garnet.

The crypt has some historic tombs and about a hundred years ago a whole book was written about it. Among the archbishops who are buried here is that Walter who founded the present cathedral and is erroneously called "Offamilio" and "Of the Mill", and therefore believed to have been English. A notable sepulchre is that of Archbishop Paternò, by Antonello Gagini; others have, in the time-honoured fashion, appropriated palaeo-Christian or classical sarcophagi, even those with pagan representations, and repose in them like venerable cuckoos. A feature one sees only rarely—

I remember another in Córdoba, Spain—is the portrayal of a dwelling on the side of the sarcophagus, with the door permanently ajar, possibly suggesting an easy passage for the occupant on the day of resurrection. It was once said that Bishop Odo, half-brother of William the Conqueror, also rested here, and some authors have repeated this belief. There is, however, no foundation for it and the occupant of every tomb has been identified.

The Archbishop's Palace, a baroque, three-storey building continuous with the campanile, on the Via M. Bonello, houses the Diocesan Museum, consisting mostly of fragments salvaged from the cathedral during alterations and from churches destroyed during the last war. The paintings are not exceptional; that of Saint Antony, however, by Vincenzo degli Azzani, gives an amusing example of how errors accumulate in religious legends. The saint's emblem in art, from the end of the fourteenth century, was a pig wearing a bell, and popular belief made it into a pet which relieved the owner's loneliness. In actual fact the emblem came about through the activities of the Antonine Hospitallers of the eleventh century; the Order spread through France and had police protection and their pigs, wearing a bell for easy recovery, being allowed to feed in the gutter, a privilege denied to lay pigs. The seal of the Order therefore evolved as a figure of Saint Antony accompanied by a pig wearing a bell. The second mistake, perpetrated by degli Azzani, living in the sixteenth century, transfers the bell from the pig to the saint. Vasari, painter and architect, friend of Michelangelo and author of the first biography of famous artists, is represented by two oils, "Hebrews carrying manna" and "Moses showing the shower of manna"; having seen them we are glad to learn that he was a better architect than painter. From the upper windows one has a close view of the cathedral roofs, with their line of tiled cupolas [*below*] and their decorative engaged columns, some spiral, some of plain porphyry and most of them quite unnecessary.

Almost opposite the cathedral is the Villa Bonanno, containing the inconspicuous remains of Roman houses; we shall see better elsewhere. As usual in Sicily, the word "villa" means a formal garden rather than a building. A step further along the Corso and we are in the park of the Royal

Palace (*Palazzo Reale*) of the Norman kings. The façade is practically all a seventeenth century work, but the Pisan tower at the north end and the Santa Ninfa tower in the centre preserve traces of the original building, with the usual triple-arched and blind windows. The back of the south end, by the way, seen from the steep Corso Tuköry, looks much more Norman with its interlacing blind arcades. Most visitors are rushed up to the the first floor immediately in order to see the celebrated Royal Chapel, but a pause in the three-tiered Renaissance courtyard is a moment well spent. Deputies and clerks hurry in and out of party offices like bees in a hive, their modern dress contrasting with the Norman walls that have been uncovered in the ground level arcade, and the graceful columns supporting the rows of arches. Were there nothing else to see, this alone would be worth the visit.

The Cappella Palatina, or palace chapel, was originally built as a private place of worship for the court, from 1132 to 1140, and survives as one of the world's great works of art. Overpowered by the glitter of the mosaics, most visitors carry away little else in their memories. The impact of these Sicilian mosaic interiors is indeed an experience which no description or picture can convey and which no other can equal. Having seen others in Daphni, Istanbul or Ravenna, you may not necessarily prefer the Sicilian, but you will at least concede that they are a separate art form, even though they were created by the Calogeri, artists from the same school. Possibly some of the effect is due to other factors. As Schwartz says, "His [Roger's] Palatine Chapel is the artistic symbol of the unique way of government which he evolved and of a civilization formed from the most diverse racial cultures . . ." There is the secret. A western style basilica as to the nave, a Byzantine choir, classical columns and capitals, Saracenic arches and ceiling, a Romanesque ambo with Cosmati work, a floor of *opus alexandrinum* with a stylized variation of that old, old eastern theme, the Tree of Life with confronting animals, could anything be more diverse? And like the civilization which Roger formed in the same way, it works. Perhaps the most significant fact is that, when the chapel was consecrated in 1140, Bishop Theophanes Cerameus declared it to be "a lasting monument of truly great and kingly ideals". The mosaics were not begun until 1154, so that the chapel, in its style and proportions alone and without the refulgence of those wonderful, gleaming mosaics, could arouse the admiration. And so I leave these marvels of Byzantine mosaic, standing out from their gold background, and the stalactite ceiling painted by Fatimid artists. The marble Paschal candlestick is a twelfth-century work, with a design ranging from Hellenistic at the base, through Byzantine and Romanesque to a top that looks like an eastern turban.

Even if someone cannot be found to open the ancient grille, it is possible to see something of the array of caskets with the aid of a field-glass. The pride of the collection is mentioned in the inventory of the chapel in 1309; it is typically oriental, lions devouring their prey, that old theme in ancient art from Mesopotamia to Mycenae and from Corinth to Motya. It was on the Paschal candlestick. One of the caskets' designs and lettering are of ivory set in black lacquer, and its handle and hinges are of bronze.

As you leave the chapel a column in the wall on your right, inscribed in three languages, commemorates the installation of Roger II's water clock in 1142. One floor higher a porter will conduct you to the royal apartments, but not until you have stared into the hall where the Regional Assembly of Sicily meets. To him this is the most important part of the building, for now at last Sicily is tasting something like liberty. Perhaps, too, he is taking an anticipatory revenge for the meanness of the average tourist, which gives him his sardonic smile. The Roger Room, although decorated after him, is one of the royal apartments in which the mosaic decoration has survived. Again, the motives are oriental, with confronting birds and animals, but there are hunting scenes too, the cosy domesticity contrasting with the insistence of those gorgeous mosaics downstairs to let them tell you a Bible story.

Continuing westward along the Corso, we pass under the porta Nuova, the great arch built in 1535 to welcome Charles V after the conquest of Tunis. It was struck by lightning in 1667 but the Palermitans, ignoring the Almighty's impeccable taste, rebuilt it. The street, having passed the limits of the old *kasr*, becomes Corso Calatafimi. A few hundred yards along, on the left side, is a barracks, and from inside you may see the remains of the Norman palace of La Cuba [*below*], with a weathered Arabic inscription

over a blocked doorway. Built by William II in 1180, it was one of a string of such pleasure houses, buildings that with their gardens surrounded Palermo like a pearl necklace on a beautiful woman, as one Arab traveller described it. I reproduce a photograph because the main features of all these structures are similar. By the time of William II ideas about spatial proportions had become set and the cubical* building with blind windows under a triple blind arcade was standard. To see inside, you have to go further along the Corso Calatafimi and at the appropriate private house be invited through and into the garden. The street door gives directly into the lounge, where you step reverently between china cabinets, glass cabinets and occasional tables with a load of artificial roses, tinsel flowers and oleographs to enter the bedroom, which is almost completely occupied by a large double bed and a shiny, many-doored cupboard taking up the whole of one wall. Past the kitchen and through the vegetable garden, a left turn and you are inside the Cuba, but alas, there are only bare walls and no roof, and where the damask tapestries hung, there is only your hostess's washing. Your imagination must be vivid if you can equate this desolation with the promise of that worn inscription outside, quoted in Boccaccio's *Restituta*, which read: "In the name of God, the clement and merciful, [this is the usual introduction to any Moslem announcement, from the Koran to a contract] stop and look. You will see the egregious dwelling of the glorious among the kings of the earth, William II. There is no castle worthy of him, nor are his halls sufficient . . ." and Amari read the end which he translated as ". . . and of our Lord the Messiah, one thousand and a hundred, added eighty, which have passed so joyfully [*che sono corsi tanto lieti*]." Further along the Corso, but this time on your right, you must find the entrance to the palazzo of the Cavaliere Napoli (street numbers won't help) and once there, one of the domestic staff will conduct you between palms and orange and lemon and loquat trees to the little Kiosk [*opposite*], known as the Cubula, which once stood in the gardens of the Cuba and whose ancestry I have described on page 82.

Now turn back towards Palermo and take the last road to the right before reaching the Porta Nuova. This leads you along the side of the Norman royal palace; first left and first right, a matter of a hundred yards, and you are at the entrance to the Church of San Giovanni degli Eremiti [*Col. pl. VIII(a)*]. Standing quiet and alone amidst a pleasantly casual garden of flowering shrubs and fruit trees, this ancient building, or its foundations, has seen more of Sicily's history than any other building we have visited. Saint John of the Hermits, it is called, but there is no record of any hermitage hereabouts. There was, however, a temple of Hermes in Greek times, and when the Romans took over they changed the god and made him their equivalent, Mercury. Saint Gregory the Great, in the sixth century,

* The name *Cuba* of course refers to the dome (*kubbeh*) or domes which once surmounted the building, and not to its shape.

inherited the ground from his mother Sylvia, a Sicilian heiress, and built a monastery over an older church, conveniently named after Saint Mercurius. He dedicated it to Saint John Hermetis, as the area was still named after the Greek temple, and this become corrupted to degli Eremiti; and for those who need convincing there is a narrow street opposite, typical of Old Palermo, called Via San Mercurio. The word "romantic" is usually employed when describing the church; it can equally be applied to the history of its name. Founded again in 1132 on the substructure of a mosque, with its own lands, it was frequently at odds with the canons of the Cappella Palatina, for they shared a common boundary and a common avarice for the property of the old Church of San Giorgio. This friction gave rise to one of the most remarkable frauds of all time, discovered only at the beginning of the present century, when a document written with gold ink on purple vellum and purporting to be a royal donation of 1140, was identified as a forgery, perpetrated by the canons of the Palatine Chapel.

The building itself is one of three which incorporate recognizable fragments of Saracen work, the others being the Castle of Favara and the Norman palace. This is a matter for experts to decide; for us the proportions of the building, its five faded red cupolas and its peaceful surroundings should suffice. Inside there are numerous fragments of the Moslem furnishings, Arabic inscriptions, some in Cufic and others in Naskhi script, a twelfth-century font resting on a column that was inscribed in Arabic, pieces of ornamental tile, a Hebrew inscription brought from elsewhere, a perforated stone window and a fragment of stalactite ceiling.

Having browsed around inside, but not too earnestly, go to the little cloister and sit next to a pair of the twin columns that support the arches. Note the typical blind arcade that runs above them and that we have now seen so often, the unobtrusive vegetation and the covered well in the centre with its creeper. If you have selected the right side you can bask in the sun while you recapture the mood of a mediaeval monastery and, raising your eyes, catch a glimpse of a rosy cupola. There is always something new to be found in this garden; last time I was there I came upon a fragment of wall with a twin window separated by the most delicate marble column imaginable. Luckily the Spaniards, whose hatred of Islam was a part of life itself when they came here and who wrecked what remained of the mosque, found nothing to offend them in the garden.

12 *In and Around Palermo*

We have wandered along the main artery of the city and seen the more obvious and important tourist attractions. Much remains, however, and though the city has grown vastly its expansion has been northward, leaving the older parts untouched, except by the Allied bombers. The Quattro Canti stands, and the four divisions of the town still meet here as they have done since Moslem days; they vary, of course, in interest and squalor, and the obvious foreigner can still be jostled and tripped up, to find an empty handbag or pocket when the group has dispersed. The four quarters are no longer rigidly allocated to races or trades and, with one exception, their names are of no importance. But wandering through the parts that have not been cleared by town planners or bombs, one can still picture the city when Brydone visited it in 1770 and found only one inn, and that with an ugly French landlady. Here came the lackey of Prince Palagonia, some ten years later, approaching passers-by for contributions to the fund for liberating Christian prisoners in the Barbary states. Goethe asked a shopkeeper who was watching the scene why the Prince, whose grotesque mansion at Bagheria still attracts visitors, could not devote the money he spent on those monstrosities to the cause for which he was collecting.

"It is always the way," said the shopkeeper; "we pay willingly for our follies but others have to supply the money for our virtues." Which contains more wisdom than the rest of Goethe's *Italian Journey*.

To see something of the north-eastern quarter we leave the Corso between the Quattro Canti and the Cala, going north along the broad Via Roma. About 600 yards further, on the left, and just past the blatantly enormous post office of the Fascist era, we come to the Museo Nazionale Archeologico. Our object, I must sometimes remind myself, is to follow History's footsteps, and here indeed we may do so and in fact trace them back to pre-history. Passing a few Punic and Egyptian inscriptions we enter the larger courtyard, once a monastery cloister, where we should pause to drink in the freshness of trees, flowers and the papyrus pool, shake off the hubbub of the street and be ready for the witnesses of other days. It is customary to hurry through and see the metopes of Selinus and, until this has been done, visitors will find difficulty in paying attention to other exhibits. They are beautifully displayed and, standing between their triglyphs, give one an approximate idea of their original appearance, except, of course, for the fact that no one has dared to colour them as they once were

117

coloured. They are a mixed lot, from various temples and from different times over the century that followed 550 B.C.; even the amateur who has never seen a metope can distinguish the earliest from the latest and amuse himself by equating the tableaux with the legends given in the guide books. We have been to Selinunte and know something of its history. We can only marvel that systematic attempts at excavation, apart from desultory digs in the fourteenth century, should have had to wait for three Englishmen: Fagan, the British consul-general, made some unsuccessful attempts in 1809, and in 1822 Harris and Angell, camping in the ruins, succeeded in finding the first series of metopes and preserving them for our delight. The metopes cannot be described; either you see them or else study the many excellent reproductions in art books: words cannot help, "not even", as Homer sang, "if I had ten tongues and ten mouths".

On the first floor is the celebrated bronze ram from the Castello Maniace in Syracuse, originally one of a pair of Hellenistic castings. Goethe admired its extraordinarily life-like appearance in fulsome terms, apparently forgetting that earlier in the same book he had written: "... the crowd, whose artistic judgement consists solely in finding the imitation like the original." We are apt to be too kind to earlier travel writers; Goethe himself was indebted to Patrick Brydone, whose letters to William Beckford were written during a journey in Sicily ten years earlier. Neither of them paid much attention to what we regard as artistic marvels; nowhere does Goethe even mention the Byzantine mosaics of Palermo and Monreale. Brydone does at least remark: "The Chiesa del Pallezzo [he means the Cappella Palatina] is entirely encrusted over with ancient mosaic; and the vaulted roof too is all of the same.—But it is endless to talk of churches." He found time to talk, nevertheless, of the production of *paté de foie gras* in Agrigento and of the method of tunny fishing which is still in use today. The twin rams had a wandering life; they first appear in history when the Castle of Maniace in Syracuse was built, by Frederick II and not, as some believe, by George Maniakes. The Marquis of Gerace fancied them in 1448 and took them to Castelbuono, but when the family goods were confiscated later they came to Palermo. After trying various homes they were housed in the Norman palace, where Goethe admired them. But in the revolution of 1848 one of them was damaged by a bomb and then melted down for munitions. The more we read of man and his history, the more we marvel, not at what has been destroyed, but at how much has survived.

It is not far from the museum to the Church of Sant' Agostino, still to the north of the Corso. The original doorway is true Chiaramontine work, its decoration enhanced by the tasteful contrast of black lava blocks. The rose window above, the most beautiful in Palermo, is of a somewhat later date. The side doorway is by Domenico Gagini, of whom we shall hear again, and the stucco figures inside are by Serpotta, whose extraordinary genius in the plastic arts is displayed in profusion in this city; you must make up your own mind about him, for some who admire his skill consider his products too winsome for words. Here there is a palaeo-Christian sarcophagus of a type that was common in the fourth and fifth centuries, with Christ represented in the Hellenistic manner as a beardless youth and, in the role of philosopher, carrying a scroll; the peacocks, as elsewhere in Christian art, symbolize immortality and this is founded on an old belief that the peacock's flesh does not decay.

On the way back it is worth stopping at the little Museo del Risorgimento, where Garibaldi's liberation of Sicily is commemorated. Perhaps the most interesting feature is a painting that shows the almost Messianic role that he played in the life of the common man; in it his garlanded portrait hangs on the wall, and before it one little girl holds a candle and the other kneels in prayer. Other relics of those great days can be seen in the Pepoli Museum of Trapani, where the original uniform of a local Garibaldian is displayed alongside the flag of the *Lombardo* which carried him when the Thousand came to Sicily.

Logically, we should have remained on the north side of the Corso and made our way to the famous palace of La Zisa, the Splendid. Its splendour, however, is diminishing as the Board of Works keeps it closed for restoration; I have seen the caretaker's family grow up while the palace remains closed, and the little girl who use to reach up to the keyhole is now a grown woman. Inside, the dust lies ever more thickly, obliterating frescoes and mosaics, and filling the channel through the great hall where running water once challenged the baking heat outside. For much the same reason I am not describing the Palace of La Favara, beyond the southern suburbs; what we have seen already is far more evocative of the splendour of the Norman court.

The Church of Saint Mary of the Chain introduced us to the Kalsa quarter in the last chapter; we return now to glean some more of History's leavings. The huge Piazza Marina, of which the Garibaldi gardens now occupy the greater part, was once an inlet of the sea, from the Cala. Later, as the sea receded, the large open space was used for processions, jousts, executions and other amusements. An interesting echo of the foreign influences that have been at work here is given by the three churches which cluster round—S. Maria della Catena, S. Maria di Porto Salvo and S. Maria dei Miracoli, in which experts claim to recognize not only Renaissance but Byzantine, Gothic and Catalan influences as well. All around here are the decayed remains of the old aristocratic quarter, no doubt the direct successor of the dwellings that rose round the great Saracen castle, *el Khalis*, the pure. Judging by the evidence of building styles, showing no new palaces after the middle of the seventeenth century, it seems as though the aristocracy moved to the north-western quarter of Palermo at about that time. It is probably relevant that a specially severe epidemic of plague raged in Sicily in 1642 and that famine followed in 1646, so that multitudes of peasants flocked to the towns in search of a livelihood. As still happens when an urban population rises through a flood of indigent immigrants, palaces become tenements and older residents become subject to a centrifugal impulse.

The Chiaramonte Palace was originally called the Castle, and not without reason. It was begun, apparently on the site of the old Customs House, in 1307, when the great barons took advantage of the disorders following the War of the Vespers to enrich themselves and even to usurp royal privileges. Inevitably there was bloody strife and it was the Chiaramonti who came off best. It is not surprising, therefore, to observe that the ground floor originally had no windows and that the bulk of the building reminds one of a fortress. The upper floors, however, sport the beautiful biforate and triforate windows under their ornamental Gothic arches, a typically Sicilian feature. The Siculo-Norman and Chiaramontine styles can be readily identified by the amateur; it is only in Sicilian Renaissance and Baroque that the expert eye is needed. A few moments spent in the Garibaldi gardens opposite, under the great banyan tree (*ficus indica*) with its aerial roots, studying details of the palace's façade, will not be wasted. After the fall of the Chiaramonti, when Andrea had been beheaded by Martin of Aragón in 1392, the Hosterium—Lo Steri as it is now called—became a royal and then a viceregal residence, then the headquarters of the Inquisition and finally the Law Courts.

Undoubtedly one of Sicily's greatest artistic treasures, the ceiling paintings of the great hall and an adjoining room repay careful study. We know that they were produced by Simone da Corleone, Cecco di Naro and Darenu of Palermo between 1377 and 1380, which was during the height of the Chiaramonte power, but I doubt whether the Spanish *mudéjar* style plays as important a part as one is led to believe. Certainly many of these 500 panels represent classical themes which were quite foreign to *mudéjar* art, as were whimsical themes such as that of the recumbent turtle playing the bagpipes. The subjects embrace scenes from the Old Testament, the Trojan war and the Arthurian and Carolingian cycles. In passing, one should remember that the last are still very much alive in Sicilian folk-lore and can be seen any day pictured on the Sicilian *carretta*, the ubiquitous two-wheeled cart, and form the main subjects of the puppet plays. But there are many paintings on the ceilings which are quite unconnected with these subjects. One portrays a white-bearded man, complete with bridle, being ridden by a young woman who is obviously dissatisfied with his speed, for she is using her slipper as a whip on his hindquarters; watching them from a balcony are two men, of whom one seems to point with scorn at the strange couple. The legend is one which figures in religious art in France as early as the thirteenth century; the bearded man is Aristotle, tutor of Alexander the Great, and the young woman is an Indian courtesan named Campaspe. Her name, by the way, has survived in our own literature thanks to John Lyly's play *Campaspe*. Alexander was very much in love with the Indian, and Aristotle deemed it his duty to oppose the adventure; with feminine guile Campaspe made herself so attractive to the old philosopher that, in order to prove his love, he allowed himself to be saddled and bridled. While Campaspe was riding him Alexander (who is on the balcony) observed them and the old man, though he may have looked a fool, at least used the situation to impart the precept: "How greatly should a young prince mistrust love when he sees how an old philosopher may be ensnared."

Another panel is also quite foreign to *mudéjar* art and unrelated to the cycles previously mentioned. It shows two hairy men, their tongues protruded and their advanced left arms protected by cloaks, advancing on each other with raised clubs. The Hairy Man, or Woodwose, is a common subject in church imagery and in later heraldry, where a pair is frequently shown as supporters to a coat-of-arms; according to M. D. Anderson he seems to have been considered as a good beast, although in classical literature he is associated with fauns, the prototypes of devils. Thus Cohn describes the Wild Man of mediaeval demonology as a monster of erotic and destructive power—an earth spirit originally of the family of Pan, the fauns, satyrs and centaurs. Melchior Lorch, in 1545, pictured the Pope as a Woodwose, Saint Peter's key in his left hand and the triple papal cross in his right; part of the accompanying verse, which was dedicated to Martin Luther, reads: "The Pope is rightly called the Wild Man." * The protruded tongues are realistic, if rude, and can be found elsewhere in the art of the people, if not in that of the court. At Erice, for example, in one group of the *Misteri* at Sant' Orsola the figure of an onlooker, probably meant to represent a Jew though dressed as a Saracen, has the tongue protruded while he watches Christ's Passion.

Just behind the palace is the tiny twelfth-century chapel of Saint Antony Abbott, with marble door jambs of Byzantine type, that is with reliefs of the vine tendril and alternate leaves and bunches of grapes. There are two angels as well, one with a bell and the other a pig, an interesting elaboration of the theme I described in the last chapter. On the far side of the Villa Garibaldi—villa means garden in Sicily—and a short distance along the Via Merlo is the Church of San Francesco d'Assisi, formerly part of a huge convent. It was first begun in 1234 but either building was interrupted or the church was demolished on the orders of the Emperor Frederick, whose sympathies lay with the Cistercians, perhaps because, being French, they paid less attention to the popes' frequent excommunications. In any case it was rebuilt in 1302, and obviously Sant' Agostino was used as a model; it is therefore unnecessary to study the façade in detail but it is interesting to observe how the clustered modern street lamps outside have enhanced its beauty. Inside, it shows a mixture of styles and serves as an introduction to Sicily's best known sculptures. The minute but perfect Calvello Chapel is cited as a summary of Chiaramontine art, with its Norman apse, Suevic

* *"Der Babst heist recht der Wilde Man ..."*

121

vault and inlaid geometric patterns in black and white, reminiscent of the external apsidal decorations of the cathedrals of Palermo and Monreale. All the Gothic chapels were transformed into the style of the Renaissance by Domenico Gagini and Giorgio da Milano; the former, who came from Lombardy, founded his atelier in Palermo and among the graduates of this *bottega* were at least ten other Gaginis. Domenico and Francesco Laurana, the other great pioneer of Sicilian sculpture, left Naples in 1458 to escape the tumult that followed the death of Alfonso the Magnanimous; Laurana went to the Provence and only later moved on to Palermo. Gagini left comparatively little, if we except attributions, but one of his finest works, the Madonna del Socorso, is in this church.

Laurana is also represented here, first by the sarcophagus with the recumbent figure of Antonio Speciale, a member of one of the ruling families and praetor of Palermo; there are no contrived effects, the dead man is not praying nor leaning on one elbow to read. He is simply dead, but not too dead. Anticipating, I would have you compare this effigy with the same man's bust in the National Gallery, sculptured by Domenico Gagini and allegedly influenced by Laurana. Here again there is the art which conceals art; the subject is neither haughty nor humble, stern or genial. He is just alive—only just.

But the finest memorial to the Dalmatian Laurana in this church is the carved arch of the Mastrantonio Chapel, dated 1468. Among the many reliefs is that of the two bishops at the lectern; apart from the faultless characterization of the studious faces, the hands, though unobtrusive, are as expressive as anything I can recollect. Unprejudiced examination of the works of the two sculptors will, I think, dispose of the belief that either of them influenced the other; Bottari in fact traces Gagini's education back to Florence, where he assisted with the finishing of the famous Ghiberti doors in the Baptistery.

Adjoining the Church of Saint Francis is the little Oratorio della Compagnia di San Lorenzo, where the lover of Serpotta can admire what is probably the best and most varied collection of his works. Though considered at his best in the portrayal of cherubic children or *putti*, he also shows here what he can do with grown-ups. For the unimpressed, the advantage of this collection is that they can turn away with the comforting thought "Well, we've done Serpotta". No one, by the way, knows how the disembodied, winged heads of children came to be called cherubs. Those of the Old Testament and Revelations are usually winged animals, some with four faces, and from the descriptions we have appear to be descended from the genii of pagan storm clouds.

The Palazzo Abbatelli houses the Galleria Nazionale di Sicilia, the leading art exhibition in the island, and is only a short distance away, near the Chiaramonte Palace. The name itself is open to doubt, and many authorities prefer it to the other name, Patella, assuming the latter to be a corruption. It is known, however, that a certain master-pilot of Palermo named Francesco Patella used his ill-gotten wealth to have this mansion built by Sicily's greatest architect, Matteo Carnelivari; between 1526 and 1943 it was greatly altered by Dominican nuns and bombs, but has now been well restored and is an excellent example, especially the courtyard, of the influence of the Renaissance on Catalan Gothic.

Viewing the collection with the eye of a historian, the first items are the ceramics, among which is a celebrated Hispano-Moresque vase decorated with Cufic characters, though centuries after this style of writing gave place to the Naskhi; it certainly came from Andalusia and probably from Málaga. As it is of the fourteenth century there is no need to imagine commercial interchange between Saracen countries, though it did indeed exist; this example was brought by the Spaniards. Other ceramics include the majolica of Collesano, a small town in the Madonie mountains, which presumably has carried on the tradition since Moslem days. These examples are of the sixteenth century; Palermo copied them a hundred years later and one of these latter specimens, of 1687, is signed by Filippo Rizzuto. Today the centre for majolica ware has moved to Caltagirone, in the south-east.

The great fresco, The Triumph of Death, deservedly arrests the visitor, as do the paintings of various schools displayed on the first floor. For historic interest Laurana's bust of Eleanor of Aragón claims our attention which in any case would have been bestowed on its beauty. While visitors rhapsodize over Laurana's genius, his economy of detail, the accentuation of surfaces and the overall simplicity which conveys more than a wealth of modelling, few pause to reflect that this beautiful lady, daughter of Ferdinand I of Naples, was Duchess of Ferrara and mother of the brilliant Beatrice and Isabella d'Este, a grandmother of Sforzas and Gonzagas and thus a maker of history. As for the experts who like to trace someone's influence in everyone's work, it is sufficient that Laurana was a pupil of the great Piero della Francesca.

Here you can also allegedly see the earliest evidence of Spanish influence, a part of a Catalan retablo of the Last Supper by Jaume Serra of Barcelona, dated to between 1360 and 1370. This at least is what the books say; in fact the Serra brothers were notable in Spain for introducing the Italo-Gothic style, so that we are practically back where we started. The retablo itself is of the greatest interest for its details. Christ and three of the apostles are redheads and Saint John, whose traditional leaning on the Saviour's bosom has gone so far as to rest his head right across His part of the table, is a blond. Judas is one of the redheads and the only apostle with a Semitic cast of countenance, which is clearly shown as he rather rudely stretches across the table to the central dish. Serra did not forget one detail that so many artists have overlooked; Judas Iscariot is the only one without a halo.

Sicily's greatest painter, Antonello da Messina, made history by introducing oil painting to Italy; even had he not done so he would rank among the greatest artists, and one of his finest works, the Annunciation, is in this gallery.

Going south, we reach the heart of the somewhat unsavoury quarter of Kalsa, whose piazza marks the site of the original Saracen castle of Khalis, the Pure. Nearby are the restored Church of La Magione, previously mentioned in connection with the Teutonic Order, and that of Santa Maria della Vittoria, which used to preserve an oak door charred when Robert Guiscard stormed the city in 1071. The palace of Aiutamicristo, of the late fifteenth century, has gone down in the world but still preserves portions of a magnificent courtyard; but it is difficult to imagine its splendour in 1535 when the Emperor Charles V stayed here. Another of Carnelivari's masterpieces, its cry for assistance, "*Aiutamicristo*—Help me, Christ!" seems to be going unanswered. Turning east along the broad Via Lincoln, the Botanical Gardens are on our right, and beyond them the Villa Giulia, a public garden first opened in 1777 and never modernized. Thus one can shelter in any of four Pompeian *prospetti* grouped in a highly artificial manner round a fountain, or wander beneath the orange trees, laden with fruit until well into May. Poppies are here, in more shades than the colourman could produce, marigolds, wistaria, marguerites, arum lilies and creeping lilac with pink buds and white flowers. Here, and in the adjoining garden of sub-tropical species, is a bewildering tangle of stone pine, palms, bamboo, bananas and papyrus.

Goethe, whom I have mentioned disparagingly, may have sat here, and

tradition has it that this garden provided the inspiration for the celebrated poem in *Wilhelm Meisters Lehrjahre*: "*Kennst du das Land ...*", whose French translation "*Connais tu le pays ...*" is the most popular aria in Ambroise Thomas' *Mignon*. Everything he described is here: the oranges glowing in the dark foliage, the silent myrtle and the laurel tall, the gentle breeze wafted from the blue sky. What a pity that his time in Palermo was taken up chiefly with the grotesques of the Palagonia mansion and a search for the indigent relations of the swindler Cagliostro.

Whether or not you visited the gardens, you can turn south from the Via Lincoln along the Corso dei Mille—the Street of the Thousand, until you reach the scene of their first encounter when they took Palermo from the Bourbon troops. This is the Ponte dell' Ammiraglio, the bridge erected by George of Antioch in 1113. The river Oreto has been diverted and the lovely old bridge [*left*] stands somewhat forlornly in its neglected bed, used as the neighbourhood's rubbish dump. So this bridge made history, over 700 years after it was built; for its capture led to the taking of Palermo, the biggest event of the decade and the prelude to a united Italy. To many of us it is only a trivial detail of a confused past, but at the time it was important enough for Eber, correspondent of the London *Times*, to join Garibaldi's army, and for Dumas to arrive by yacht less than two weeks later.

A little further and we reach another of those domed Norman churches, of the style of San Cataldo and San Giovanni degli Eremiti. This one is San Giovanni dei Lebbrosi (Saint John of the Lepers), said to have been built in

1071, during the siege of Palermo by Robert Guiscard and his brother, Count Roger [page 125]. Recent excavations show that the whole area was a great Saracen fort, inside which the church was presumably built. The interior is austere, though the sanctuary is relieved by the Saracen device of columns in niches at the angles. The ceiling, or at least the cross beams, are painted in oriental fashion but only one of them is original. The same applies to the handsome bronze lamps.

Our last call is to a church that lies in a different direction and for which a special trip is necessary. It is the Church of Santo Spirito, or Church of the Vespers as it is more usually called since the episode mentioned earlier. I don't know why it should be described as gloomy, for its exterior decoration is quite lively. It was built by Archbishop Walter, incorrectly called Offamilio, in 1173, and strikes an original note, for Palermo, in having the voussoirs of the window arches striped. The triple apse is fairly simple and shows the characteristic billet moulding and interlacing round arches. The plainness of the interior depends to a large extent on the undecorated stone piers and absence of capitals, but the ceiling has some interesting paintings, some of them original, and including such secular subjects as an elephant and a mermaid. The pierced stone windows with their Arabic designs show up particularly well in the clerestory and seen from inside impart an oriental touch to the Norman interior.

13 *Monreale*

The Cathedral of Monreale, which lies on the spur of a mountain five miles from Palermo, should rank as one of the wonders of the world. Goethe did not mention it; Brydone simple stated, incorrectly, that it was nearly the same size as the one at Palermo "and the whole is encrusted with mosaic, at an incredible expense". Today's tourist is rushed up in a bus, gets a quick glimpse of the doors, a slower one of the interior and a breather in the cloister; plenty of time is then allowed him for buying souvenirs and postcards. The discerning amateur will allow himself a whole morning, for not only will he see a combined exhibition of architecture and mosaic, but also two of the world's few remaining Romanesque bronze doors and a cloister whose carved capitals alone could consume some days if all of them were to be "read".

The cathedral is called Santa Maria la Nuova, for it was new when completed in 1176. The ostensible reason for its construction, so near to the huge cathedral of Palermo which was being built at the same time, was the discovery by William II of a treasure, whose whereabouts was revealed to him in a dream by the Virgin. The episode forms the subject of a painting in the adjacent college, by Giuseppe Velazquez; this painter, by the way, was no relation to the great Velazquez, court painter to the Spanish king, and for two reasons: first, Giuseppe's real name was Velasco and secondly, the great Velazquez's patronymic was De Silva. The real reason for the building of Monreale was political. During William's minority supreme power fell into the hands of the Archbishop Walter who built Palermo cathedral and the Church of the Vespers; an opposing faction was led by Walter's vice-chancellor, Matthew of Ajello. Condensing the story, the king himself, on coming of age, felt that Walter's power needed curtailing, and in order to bring this about he founded a Benedictine abbey, had an ornate church built and endowed it with extensive territories and privileges, many of them at the expense of Palermo's archbishopric. Walter had come to power amid violence; there is a hint that the royal party was mindful of this in the fact that the young king kept the building plan secret, saying that he intended putting up only a simple Benedictine abbey. The site selected was the Mons Regalis, the royal mountain on which Roger II had built a castle in a park, and whose name soon became Monreale; the church, as it was at first, was erected over the site of a small chapel called Hagia Kyriaka, not from an imaginary Saint Kyriaka, but because the word means Sunday, and the chapel was thus distinguished from the old cathedral of Palermo, which became a mosque and thus became known as the Friday church.

The abbey was built on the site of the village of Bulchar, and the seminary now adjoining the transept was originally the royal castle. The architecture shows Campanian influence, with its taste for polychrome decoration; there is also a suggestion of the Pisan style, and we know that relations with Pisa were particularly cordial, ever since the Pisan fleet offered to help Guiscard and Roger I in the siege of Palermo; an offer, incidentally, which was refused. The interior, too, to anticipate, is essentially a repetition of the Montecassino of Desiderius and the cathedral of Salerno, with a narthex and a cloister on the south side, on to which the buildings look.

The cathedral's exterior gives little promise of the glories to be found inside. The western façade, now closed by railings, is spoiled by a horrible eighteenth-century porch which has taken the place of the old narthex. One of the towers has been lost and the beautiful bronze doors can be seen only from the railings; we shall come back to them. The apse, even more beautiful than that of Palermo cathedral, follows the same pattern of interlacing arches, medallions of various design, and polychrome workmanship through the use of different types of stone [*opposite*]. Strangely enough, though the overall effect is that of Saracen work, each individual feature can be duplicated in western art. When you return to the western face, in order to examine the bronze doors, note by the way that there are traces of crenellation on the remains of the north tower and arrow slits instead of windows in some parts.

The great western doors were signed by the artist, Bonanno de Pisa, in 1186. They represent one of the early examples of a new technique in this department of church decoration, for previous doors had been cast exclusively in Constantinople, in the niello technique, which entailed engraving the design on bronze and subsequently filling with silver. It was only in the twelfth century that the technique of casting in relief, which we see here, was invented in southern Italy or Sicily. Bonanno had won a reputation for this sort of work by making the doors of Pisa cathedral in 1180; he had also begun to build the Leaning Tower of Pisa, in association with one William, in 1173. His reputation was not apparently affected when the tower began to lean. Two interesting details emerge from a study of these superb doors: first, it can be shown that the doors were ordered by letter and that the measurements provided were not accurate, for one can see the adjustments that had to be made to accommodate them to the Siculo-Norman portal. Secondly, one of the panels, that of the Nativity, which is sixth from the top and second from the right, has the legend in mirror writing. It is tempting to believe that the whole panel was cast as a negative; the fact that one of the midwives holds a jug in the right hand would suggest that this is not so, but the angels hold their staffs in their left hands; perhaps this is only because

the artist used the nearer limb when small details had to be represented. So far as I know, no serious attempt has been made to explain the mirror writing. The north doors, at the present entrance to the cathedral, are by Barisano da Trani and antedate the others, having been cast in 1179; this artist also made the surviving bronze doors of Trani and Ravello, and it is interesting to observe that many of the panels appear in more than one of these three churches, showing that Barisano had permanent moulds from which identical bronze panels could be produced.

However much your reading may have prepared you, the impact of the interior is almost physical. You have seen the Capella Palatina and you feel that nothing richer could exist. Here you will confess your error. This is where the Norman kings, determined to rival the splendour of Byzantium, put in their shop window every last piece of their stock; you stand and stare in amazement at the lavish display of a resplendent art. But before examining the mosaics it is as well to get a general idea of the interior, the eighteen antique columns, only one of them of marble, the basilican plan, a western touch that contrasts with the oriental features, and the beautiful marble screen before the choir. Few have time to glance at the porphyry sarcophagus of William I or the sixteenth century marble tomb of his son, let alone the inscription that tells of the sojourn of Saint Louis's mortal remains on their way home from Tunis; an old account tells us that his bowels are buried here, and the concept is not improbable, for there was a perpetual scramble for the various limbs and organs of holy men, but if his bowels were ever here someone has moved them.

The mosaic area, to put it in cold print, is the largest of any church in the world, comprising 8,000 square feet. What that means in man-hours Heaven alone knows. The mosaics are later, both in style and date, than those in Palermo or Cefalù and, far from being the work of Sicilians trained by the Calogeri, as was once believed, they represent an artistic style which came into fashion at this time, the end of the Comnenan dynasty, in Constantinople. The same dynamic style extends through Bulgaria and Russia, which it reached at about the same time. It is therefore fairly certain that a large team of artists was hired to decorate this interior, and what the critics call debased is simply the trend to naturalism which was ousting the traditional Byzantine hieratic formality. If these mosaics seem more like a documentary record, therefore, it is because we miss the cruder but perhaps more sincere productions of earlier days; for some the primitive floor of Otranto cathedral, the striving of an earnest monk who knew nothing of Byzantine art, has a more lasting message. The mosaics of Monreale narrate the story of the world, from the Creation to the Acts of Saints Peter and Paul; as an afterthought scenes from the lives of local saints are added and there are, almost of course, illustrations of Christ crowning William II and of the latter offering the cathedral to the Virgin. Thomas à Becket is here too, within ten years of his martyrdom, a fact which astonishes many as the

Queen of Sicily at this time was the daughter of Henry II, who was held to be guilty of Thomas's murder. There may not, however, have been any need to spare her feelings; her brothers, Richard and John, at least never disguised their loathing for their father and, as Dahmus says, "Among the most zealous advocates in spreading devotion to the new saint were the three daughters of Henry II who fostered his cult in the lands of Germany, Sicily, and Spain where their husbands ruled".

Studying the Pantocrator in the apse, the majestic figure of Christ in Benediction, one is entitled to wonder whether there was friction between the Greek and Latin communities. In His left hand he holds the book with the customary text "*Ego sum lux mundi...*—I am the Light of the World", but on the opposite page the same text is written in Greek: "*Ego eimi to phos tou kosmou...*" Precisely the same can be seen in the mosaic of the Pantocrator in Cefalù, and in both the right hand, raised in blessing, has assumed a position midway between the Greek and Latin styles.

After the golden glitter of the cathedral the cloisters provide the same contrast as did the muttered breviary of the slowly pacing monks to the thundering *Kyrie eleison* of the eastern service. Here all is western, all that is except the pointed arches held up by the twin columns. But even here colour is not altogether lacking, for many of the columns have ribbons of Cosmati mosaic along or round their shafts. The capitals are the chief glory of these cloisters, and different artists can be recognized as sculptors of the 109 groups. Some experts even maintain that identical artists were employed in the Basilica of Santa Restituta in Naples. At all events the sculptors were recruited from Campania, where there was a large pool of Tuscan, Lombard, Apulian and even Provençal talent, and this may account for the resemblance of some of these capitals to others in the Île de France and especially the cathedral of Chartres.

The themes are varied and, as in so many cloisters of the twelfth century, not wholly religious by any means. It was this which prompted Saint Bernard to ask angrily, "What are these fantastic monsters doing in the cloisters, under the very eyes of the brothers as they read? What is the meaning of these unclean monkeys, these savage lions and monstrous centaurs?" The answer is that, like the flower and vegetable motifs carved on some capitals, the monsters are meant to be decorative only, and if the sculptors enjoyed creating fantastic forms, who shall blame them? One capital poses a problem: it shows a turbaned man sitting sideways on a bull and plunging a knife into its breast. Give him a Phrygian cap, a dog and a snake, and you have the well-known representation of Mithras slaying the bull, the altar piece of the religion which so nearly won the fight against Christianity in the fourth century. It seems as though the sculptor may have been ignorant of the implications of his subject, that he had seen the usual group at some time and tried to reconstruct it from memory. But even to those whose interests do not include Romanesque capitals there is something so peaceful in this cloister that the spirits of the most jaded tourist must revive—if he is allowed the necessary ten minutes. Of the so-called Moorish fountain I have nothing more to say; admire it for what it is, not for what it is said to be.

14   Syracuse—Ortygia

Syracuse was one of the earliest Greek colonies and later became the most powerful in Sicily. The island of Ortygia, which lies a stone's throw from the mainland, fulfilled all the requirements of the earliest traders: it was easily defended, well watered and provided with a safe harbour on either side of the narrow strait, so that ships could lie unharmed whatever the prevailing wind. Homer names it, but scholars, avoiding any risk to their reputations, are inclined to doubt whether his Ortygia, twice mentioned, is the same as that of Syracuse. *Ortyx* is a quail in Greek, and even today this migrating bird rests on the Aegatian Islands, at the other end of Sicily, on its journey from North Africa. Is it difficult to believe that they used the Syracusan island too, until it became populated and built over? Delos was another Quail Island and there were possibly half a dozen where the birds used to alight on their way to various parts of Europe. Whatever may be the identity of Homer's, this Quail Island was settled by Greeks as early as 733 B.C., according to Thucydides, and has remained inhabited without a break ever since. It is therefore fitting that we should visit it first, for in its small compass—about one half by one third of a mile—it contains traces of almost every epoch.

The direction of the island is north–south, and with the tongue of main-land to which it is joined by a bridge, the Ponte Nuovo, it partly closes the Great Harbour of Syracuse, which lies to the south and west. On the other side of the neck of this promontory, and communicating with the Great Harbour by the channel below the bridge, is the Little Harbour, where the ancient Syracusan Greeks had their shipyards. As we turn our backs to the mainland and cross the bridge, we can see the Darsena, as it is still called, with fishing boats on our left and freighters on the right. There is a Darsena in Alicante too, the word simply meaning a workshop or house in Arabic (compare Dar-es-Salaam). The island is densely populated and the whole of Syracuse, in fact, has filled up recently. This sudden rise in population is attributed to the immigration of Italians from the former North African colonies, of Sicilians from the interior who became wealthy, by local standards, from the sale of wheat and oil on the black market, and lastly, strange though it may sound, by visitors to the latest miracle, the Madonnina delle Lacrime, pilgrims who came to pray and remained to stay. Hence the prevailing physical type is changing; the regular Greek features and the luminous eyes of the Saracen are becoming rarer, just as it is becoming difficult to recognize in the neglected buildings with their lines of washing the characteristic local baroque fronts with their "goose breast" kneeling balconies and trailing geraniums.

But in essence Ortygia is unchanged; the little streets still wind in their old, leisurely way and the tiny cafés still serve the iced almond confection akin to the Spanish *horchata* and possibly a relic of viceregal times. One can see the cellars where salt has, from ancient days, been stored and, until recently, snow from Etna too. This, by the way, used to be exported to Italy and Malta and the monopoly belonged to the bishops of Catania. Traces of French occupation persist in the Syracusan dialect, though not to be compared with the Angevin French patois still spoken at Sperlinga. Eighty, instead of being *ottanta*, remains *quattro ventine*, or *quatre vingt*, envelope is *inviluppo* instead of *busta* and a tailor is *custurera* (*couturier*) rather than *sarto*. The cries of street vendors echo through the alleys every morning as they have done for centuries, and a peep inside many a shop or front parlour reveals a pair of ox horns, a potent averter of the Evil Eye.

From the bridge it is only a few yards to the ruins of the Temple of Apollo; dating from the late seventh or early sixth century B.C., it is certainly one of the oldest Greek temples in the world, as the two remaining, ponderous Doric columns suggest. A long and sterile argument has raged over these few remains, some maintaining that it was the Temple of Artemis (Diana) to which Cicero referred when, on the subject of Ortygia, he mentioned two temples "which far excel the rest, that of Diana and the other, the most splendid before the arrival of that man [i.e. Verres], of Minerva". Although an inscription on the top step of the east side records the name of Kleomenes and a dedication to Apollo, it does not quite settle the argument, for this god was frequently housed in the same temple as his sister Artemis. One can lean on the railings, with one's back to the bus stop, and meditate over the changes that have occurred in this once sacred precinct. In the fourth century A.D. it became a church, in the ninth a mosque, in the eleventh a church again—you can see a Norman entrance about ten feet up one wall—and later a Spanish infantry barracks until eventually the site was almost lost under a cluster of mean houses.

A broad, uninteresting street, the Via Savoia, takes us to the Great Harbour and, turning left, we leave the modern quays and docks behind and enter the Foro Italico, a beautiful waterside promenade at which private yachts still occasionally tie up, but not for long. I overheard a couple at breakfast once, as we steamed towards the Island of Cos. "What's there?" asked one, and the other, in the flat voice of one whose trials are never-ending, replied, "More ruins, I suppose." And Syracuse, however rich it may be in ruins, is short on bathing beaches and night clubs. Facing us is the Porta Marina, which led through the walls built by Charles V's command with stones, needless to say, taken from the treasures of antiquity. I have mentioned Charles before and shall not do so again; though he is remembered as ruler of the greatest empire that ever was and even had a

134

brandy named after him, to some of us he is merely the last of the Vandals. The gate is distinguished by the usual long voussoirs of the arch, here called Catalan but seen throughout the remains of sixteenth-century Spain, and by a blind window beneath the machicolations, an example of plateresque ornament which explains the origin of the term from the Spanish word *platero*, a worker in precious metal. The Foro Italico has the shade of a regiment of trees, and in front of the lofty wall on the landward side, where bougainvillæa flourishes, is a low stone parapet occupied by elderly men; is it significant that no two sit together? It is possibly relevant that gossiping is left to the females in Sicily, and even where men foregather—I am reminded particularly of depressed areas like Partinico on a public holiday—there is a noticeable absence of chatter. At the end of the Foro there is a small but attractive aquarium, a collection of the more exotic fish among whom one may recognize many an acquaintance, and then one ascends to the celebrated Fountain of Arethusa.

There are at least two legends about this nymph, whose face appears on the well-known tetradrachms and decadrachms of Syracuse [*below*]

and even the most credulous must admit that they cannot both be true. Among the Nereids, the golden-haired daughters of the Old Man of the Sea, was Arethusa. The hunter Alpheius pursued her, but she did not reciprocate his love and took refuge on the island of Ortygia, where she was changed into a spring. Alpheius, who remained near Olympia, in Greece, was himself changed into a river and his waters, crossing the sea, joined and mingled with those of Arethusa. Another version makes Alpheius a river from the start, and the first object of his love Artemis; this goddess, however,

135

succeeded in eluding him by the simple expedient of daubing herself with mud. Later, when Arethusa had become the object of the river god's affections, it was Artemis who guided her below the sea and changed her into a fountain. Here at least we have an explanation for a temple to Artemis and the fountain of Arethusa on the same small island. Pausanius, the second-century travel writer, certainly believed that the river which flows past Olympia came up in Sicily, and does not contradict the ancient belief that the blood of sacrifices in the former place appeared in the Fountain of Arethusa. The ancients mentioned this plentiful supply of fresh water often enough; it appears in the third book of Virgil's *Aeneid*, and before that Cicero describes it, along with the teeming fish, the grey mullet that prefer the fresh to their normal salt water environment. Nelson shattered the belief that large ships could not enter the Great Harbour, and watered his fleet here before finding and destroying the French fleet at Aboukir. According to his letters to the Hamiltons, he believed that he had them to thank for the liberal interpretation of the rules of neutrality by the Kingdom of the Two Sicilies. Nelson regarded the event as a good omen: ". . . surely, watering at the Fountain of Arethusa, we must have victory." Almost immediately after, one of Sicily's numerous earthquakes rendered it salt for a time, but by the beginning of this century cups were provided for those who wished to drink from it.

Today one looks over a railing at the clear water, the mullet and the various fowl that inhabit the pool. There are nesting-boxes on the walls for smaller birds and, except when they are forcibly removed elsewhere for damaging the papyrus clumps, the swans, geese and ducks live amicably together, trustfully laying their eggs on the tiny islands. The feed-boxes for the first two are on the paved walk that surrounds the pool; the ducks are humoured by having theirs a few inches below the water. It is pleasant to lean over the pool, watching the bubble of the entering spring, the delicate papyrus fronds and the activities of fish and fowl and to list in one's mind the famous men, Archias, Aeschylus, Plato, Archimedes, Marcellus, Hadrian, Belisarius, the Emperors Frederick of Hohenstaufen and Charles V of Spain, Horatio Nelson and so many others who have looked at this historic fountain and who may have drunk its waters. Even De Ruyter, the Dutch admiral who sailed up the Medway and destroyed the English fleet at Chatham, died here after a sea-fight with the French off Augusta, though it is doubtful whether he ever set eyes on the Fountain of Arethusa.

Climbing the Via Picherale we reach the Piazza del Duomo, an attractive collection of imposing façades from the sixteenth to the eighteenth centuries. Here, on the highest point of the island, the Feast of Santa Lucia delle Quaglie is celebrated on the first of May. Did you not guess that the quails would return to the scene? At this spot, where some say the quail was sacred to Athene, whose temple looms over you, flowers and quails are thrown towards the silver statue of Saint Lucy, the virgin patron saint of

Syracuse; the quails are an essential part of the ceremony and formerly the populace would try to capture them with caps or scarves. The ceremony is a reminder of one of Saint Lucy's miracles, when exhausted quails stopped during their spring migration (which supports my guess concerning the origin of the name Ortygia) and saved the famine-stricken population from death. Saint Lucy, by the way, is universally invoked against diseases of the eye, as I explained in Chapter 6, and by an extension of this belief, she is also believed to protect against the Evil Eye, of such frequent incidence in this country.

Immediately opposite the cathedral is the National Museum, one of the finest archaeological collections in the world, and a monument to two famous workers, Paolo Orsi and Bernabò Brea. It was founded in 1809 by Bishop Trigona, as a small diocesan museum, and among its first treasures was the Landolina Venus which we shall shortly see. Prehistory should not detain us long, but there used to be the skeleton of a child with rickets; it was, last time I inquired, in the custody of a local physician who is presumably trying to find out why a disease of civilization and absence of sunlight should affect a prehistoric child. It may be that he will decide that the rickets followed an affection of the kidneys and it would be interesting to know for how long humanity has been afflicted with its present diseases. Certainly a common form of spinal arthritis has been found in the skeletons of some of Alexander the Great's soldiers, but the same condition was also present in a mummified crocodile of the Pharaohs, and even in a fossilized dinosaur.

Of early Greek settlement there are finds from various cemeteries and, from the original Temple of Athene across the piazza, a Gorgon's head with its original colouring. Clay altars have the old theme of lions killing various animals, that we saw first at Motya; a headless goddess suckles twins; archaic male statues, the well-known *kouroi*, display the sculptors' knowledge of anatomy and in one case even the purpose of the statue. On the right thigh, in primitive letters that read from right to left, it declares that this funeral effigy is in honour of Sombrotidas the physician, son of Mandrocles. Classical sculpture culminates here in the famous Venus Anadyomene of Landoline, so called after its discoverer in 1804. Much has been written about this female, who holds a fold of her robe across the lower belly, while the other arm, now broken off, lay across her breasts. It is looked down on today, precisely because it is coy and alluring and because Maupassant, who knew a good bottom when he saw one, felt like pinching it. But that is probably all that the artist was striving for. So famous is this statue, and so often debated over by experts and compared with the Venus di Milo and other works, that the story is told of the old attendant, guiding a party round the museum and coming to this exhibit, with the words, in Sicilian dialect, "This, gentlemen, is the Venus di Museo."

To lovers of early Christian art, there are few works to compare with the

137

sarcophagus of Adelphia, which was discovered in Syracuse, in the cata-comb of San Giovanni. It is a late example, dating from the middle of the fourth century, of the style of reliefs on the Arch of Constantine in Rome, those, that is to say, which were not taken from older monuments, and still bears traces of vermilion paint. An inscription records that the deceased was the wife of a magistrate, Count Valerius, and their portraits appear in relief on the front. Scenes from the Old and New Testaments are liberally mixed, Adam and Eve next to the entry of Christ into Jerusalem. Christ and Moses are both shown beardless, the former with the usual philosopher's scroll; the magi as well as the three Hebrews refusing to worship the statue of Nebuchadnezzar wear the Phrygian cap of Mithras, possibly by now associated with the Orient. Intensive detective work has discovered that the sarcophagus was made in Rome, at about the middle of the fourth century, in an atelier on the Via Appia close to the catacomb of Saint Calixtus.

It is not always appreciated that the collection of ancient Sicilian coins is unique for completeness combined with beauty. For those who confuse value with cost I can only say that the display is priceless and that your tour through the coin rooms is under the eye of a very watchful guardian. Among the minor interests of this section are four Byzantine and thirty-eight Arab glass weights, as originally used by apothecaries and later, according to Professor Balog, as currency.

The cathedral of Santa Maria delle Colonne is opposite the museum and occupies a site which has been used for worship continuously since the eighth century B.C. Along the north wall, in the Via Minerva, can be seen the huge Doric columns and the stylobate of the fifth-century temple; only vestiges of previous ones were found beneath by Orsi. They say that, when this temple was built, the golden shield of Athene (equated by the Romans with Minerva) on the pediment acted as a landmark for sailors; it is doubtful whether a statue of the goddess ever stood on the roof. Thanks to the depredations of Verres and Cicero's denunciation we have some idea of the wealth that has been lavished on the temple. The inner walls were covered with paintings by Zeuxis, of a cavalry engagement between King Agathocles and the Carthaginians; the artist's reputation for realism was so great that birds were said to have pecked at the grapes he painted. Other paintings included portraits of 27 of the tyrants and kings of Syracuse, and the splendid doors, enriched with gold and carved ivory, were described by Cicero as the most magnificent in the world. The temple was probably built by Gelon as a thank-offering for the victory of Himera in 480 B.C., so that this building and the famous decadrachm represent the beginning of an artistic flowering.

It was presumably used as a church from the fourth century A.D., but the first clear record we have informs us that Bishop Zosimus, in about 640, had a proper conversion effected. Arches were opened in the walls of the *cella*, as in the Temple of Concord at Agrigento, and presumably the orientation was changed, for the Greek temple had its major access (for priests —worshippers stayed outside) at the eastern end, whereas the Christian church reversed this. But as Greek temples were almost identical at the ends, like a tramcar, the change would not entail any extra alterations.

The eighteenth-century baroque façade of the Sicilian style is handsome enough, and the gesticulating statues of Saints Peter and Paul, by Marabitti, are not out of place. As no portion of the Greek temple is visible from the front there is no clash of styles, and the change as we enter the simple but majestic interior is all the more impressive. The entrance, between the two Doric columns of the opisthodomos, brings us into what was once the *cella* and is now the nave; only the prejudice of a classical scholar will deny that the arches cut in the side walls have contributed to the majesty of the interior. Through them the original columns of the peristyle are visible, those on the left, or north side, built into the outside wall along the Via Minerva [*below*], those on the right serving to separate the three chapels

from the south aisle; [*below*] shows the extraordinary effect obtained by the contrast between the fourth and fifth columns and the wrought-iron gates. Those between the second and third columns are of bronze, by Pietro Spagnuolo, and who more suitable for this type of church decoration than Peter the Spaniard? The first chapel is actually the baptistery and contains a Norman font, cut from an inscribed Greek marble block, resting on bronze

lions [*below*]; behind it are a few remains of Cosmati mosaic and the outer door is patterned in vaguely Saracen style. Along the north wall the old Doric columns are sadly out of alignment, the result of the earthquakes of 1542 and 1693; the wheel of bells, used during the elevation of the Host, is no longer there, but this once rare device—there is one in Tarragona—is now mass-produced for the tourist trade.

The Piazza Archimede is a short distance away, in the centre of the island and, though it is a bus terminal, is a pleasant spot for just sitting and watching the life of the old city. The central fountain is handsome but not ancient, for the square came into existence only towards the end of the last century. At the south-west corner is the façade of the Palazzo Lanza with a fifteenth-century window, said to be the best in Sicily. Though I cannot understand how such comparisons can be made, I must admit that it strikes a different note from the many Chiaramontine windows we have seen. Here there is no blind arch above, with sculptured relief; instead, a simple ridge forms an arch with a central upward point, a characteristic of the Spanish Isabelline variety of late Gothic. The twin windows are shaped to produce the same effect and separated by one of the slenderest marble columns imaginable; altogether a delightful work. The other building of note, now the Banco d'Italia, used to be the "clock house" and is chiefly remarkable for the fine fifteenth century exterior staircase of Catalan style.

A short walk takes you to the best of all Ortygia's mediaeval residences, the Montalto Palace of 1397; the living quarters of the owners, as usual on the first floor or *piano nobile*, are lighted by two surviving Chiaramontine windows and below them there is a coat-of-arms and an inscription in Gothic lettering. A monumental arcaded staircase in the neglected court-yard dates from at least a century later. A pleasant stroll through old streets takes you to the eastern shore of the island, and by following the Lungomare past the attractively coloured houses you may enjoy a variety of views. At the southern end a narrow promontory reaches out towards Cape Plemmyrion and thus forms one of the pincers that enclose the Great Harbour, and about here is the Palazzo Bellomo, now a museum of mediaeval and modern art.

Our last visit on the island is to the castle at the extreme tip. Named Maniace, it was once thought to have been built by the Byzantine general who reconquered Syracuse, but the whole plan and every detail of the architecture tell us that it was of the Suevic pattern introduced by the Emperor Frederick after his return from his crusade. We may not be altogether justified in denying that George Maniakes had a castle on this site, or that Roman and Greek ones preceded it, as the inhabitants still maintain; it would indeed be strange if a situation such as this, commanding the harbour entrance and protecting Ortygia, had no fortification. The castle consists of a massive square with cylindrical corner towers and shows a great resemblance to the castles constructed in the east under the Omayyad dynasty. Experts believe it was built by men from the Cistercian workshops, which were at that time deserted; we saw in Palermo how the Church of Saint Francis had to wait for the end of the Hohenstaufens before it could be completed: the Cistercian church of Murgo, between Augusta and Catania, is still unfinished. Your guide, for the castle is now a part of the barracks and you have to be under military escort, takes you through the Gothic portal with its black-and-white striped voussoirs and Corinthian capitals, all of marble. It is not often that one finds mediaeval capitals—and the same applies to those we shall see within—of such pure classical design, and one may well feel that Frederick, who styled himself Augustus and had the portrait on his coinage modelled on that of Roman emperors, felt that these capitals were more in keeping with his role.

On either side of the arch are the empty ledges that housed the Hellenic bronze rams whose survivor we saw in the Palermo Museum. The courtyard is now unroofed, presumably by the powder magazine explosion of 1704, but before that must have looked like a large Cistercian basilica. Here is the same strength and simplicity, and traces of the great arches that sprang from the engaged columns and pilasters. The fireplace is on a scale to match these splendours and helps to complete the mental picture of a mediaeval hall of the grandest kind. A spiral, covered staircase leads to the flat roof. Strolling here, where the stumpy lighthouse stands, one can envy the keeper's family, to whom the glorious views of the Sicilian coast, the Great Harbour and the huddle of Ortygia are available without expense or effort. They would probably give their souls to live in Detroit.

15   *Syracuse—The Mainland*

The Greeks originally distinguished the mainland Syrakousai, which took its name from the Syrako marshes of the River Anapo, from the island of Ortygia. Its area is many times greater than that of the island and it supported an enormous population; it is impossible to give even an approximate number of inhabitants, as ancient writers, like some of us today, put effect before accuracy. We may at least get an idea by contemplating what is left of the enormous circuit of the walls, and not least by the remains of the theatre, the largest in Sicily and, in its final form, capable of accommodating over fifteen thousand spectators. From the Ponte Nuovo, with one's back to Ortygia, one sees the mainland as a flat, built-up foreground, backed by a ridge that runs westward from the sea coast at a point about a mile to the north-east. We know that the city was repeatedly ravaged by epidemics from early times, and at least some of the ancients found higher ground to be healthier; it is not surprising, therefore, that the chief remains of classical times are situated on the ridge and that the intervening low ground, the Achradina of the Greeks, is of little interest to the archaeologist.

The ridge was the site of two further civic areas, Tyche, so named after the Temple of Fortune that used to stand there, and Neapolis, or New Town, which is the principal archaeological zone. Of all its monuments the theatre is perhaps the most difficult to miss and gives us glimpses of many centuries of history. Like all Greek theatres, it is built into a hillside, in this case using that called Temenites from the fact that it supported the temple and sacred precinct (*temenos*) of Apollo. The original, wooden theatre occupied the lowest part of the present one, as it had to be grouped around one of the few stretches flat enough to be used as orchestra. Remembering my remarks in an earlier chapter, you will wonder how the primitive auditorium escaped being flooded by storm water; we can only presume that drains were cut to conduct this away, exactly as they were cut to protect the present, much enlarged theatre, where they can easily be identified. The sixth-century prototype saw the works of at least one famous playwright, Epicharmus, who has the distinction of first introducing a plot into his comedies, a custom that lasted until quite recently.

The second and somewhat larger stone theatre was built by Hieron I in about 475 B.C., that is about five years after the twin victories of Salamis and Himaera, and it is quite likely that its construction was in the nature of a thanksgiving for, as we know, theatrical performances were a religious rite. It is therefore appropriate that one of the first plays presented was the patriotic *Persians* of. Aeschylus. By this time the population had grown sufficiently for the new theatre to be twice as large as its predecessor and accommodate an audience of more than six thousand. The third version was the work of Hieron II in about 230 B.C. and this is roughly what we see today, allowing for additions by the Romans and subtractions by the Spaniards. There is an ambulatory about half way to the *cavea*, and carved in it in bold Greek letters are the names of those to whom the various sections were dedicated; those that survive comprise Zeus Olympios, King Hieron, his wife Philistis, whose coins we have already seen, and Queen Nereis, Hieron's daughter-in-law and daughter of Pyrrhus. Though sadly mutilated, this huge stone shell still enables one to picture the scene, when the auditorium was packed with spectators through the livelong day, as play after play was presented, every word considered and appreciated, greeted with applause or cat-calls, or even with showers of stones; the reactions, in fact, of an intelligent crowd that has nothing to read and two theatrical festivals a year to enjoy.

Many events other than the drama were staged here. Important public questions were debated in public, and guides used to show the credulous where blind Timoleon's litter was placed when he had relinquished the dictatorship and continued to state his views as a private citizen. An old tale states that the non-combatants gathered in the theatre to watch the battle in the Great Harbour, when the Athenian navy suffered its last, catastrophic defeat. Others had been endured in the previous weeks, notably that which the Syracusans won by having their lunch brought down to the seashore; the Athenians were unprepared for such a drastic shortening of the usual lunch hour and were surprised in every sense during the afternoon. The last fight was simply the culmination of a series of such reverses and one senses from Thucydides's narrative that the morale of the Athenians was so low that they considered the mastery of the sea to have been lost while they still had a superiority in numbers. Whether the Syracusans could have watched the battle from the theatre as it was in 414 B.C. is doubtful and depends on the height of the stage and its permanent fittings; the point is not an important one. A far more dramatic episode occurred here only a short time after, when the captured Athenian generals, Nicias and Demosthenes, were condemned to death in this theatre, in spite of the pleadings of Gylippus, leader of the Spartan contingent, to whom the unfortunate Nicias had personally surrendered. And since 1914 there has been a triennial performance of Greek plays here, but not as the Greeks used to see the actors, all males, with masks and *cothurni*; the first play was the *Agamemnon* of Aeschylus, and for twentieth-century ears it was perhaps as well that Clytemnaestra and Cassandra were not baritones.

On the other side of the Greek theatre is the largest and most accessible of the famous stone quarries of Syracuse, the Latomia del Paradiso. Being

well within the archaeological zone it is most convenient for guides, who pretend that it was here the 7,000 Athenian prisoners were left to languish for eight months, with a daily dole of corn and water, no sanitation and the putrefying corpses of their more fortunate comrades. The actual site does not matter much, but it is as well to point out that this *latomia* is hemmed in by its precipitous walls on three sides only and that the prisoners would have needed stricter supervision here than in other quarries. Most of the surviving Athenians were eventually sold into slavery and very few ever found their way back to Greece; a few, and it is said that they were the ones who could quote verses from Euripides—so avid of culture were the Syracusans—were released, for in those days the spirit could still on occasion rise above man's innate passions. Speaking of the theatre, Nelson-Hood clothed the episode in words worthy of the occasion: "Here rang out the words of Euripides, the plaint of the Trojan women, the beauty of which so moved their Syracusan conquerors that the Athenian prisoners, slowly starving to death, gained tardy deliverance from bondage in the fateful quarries." Today we can try to forget the misery of those unfortunates as we wander through the beautiful tropical gardens that flourish in the sheltered depth of the quarries. Here the trees rise to prodigious heights as each strives to outstrip its neighbours and offer its leaves to the life-giving sun; as you wander in their shelter you may well imagine yourself in Avilion, "where falls not hail, or rain, or any snow, nor ever wind blows loudly"; and the only discords are the ugly voices of the guides and their flocks, bleating their "halloas" as loudly as they can into the Ear of Dionysus [*opposite*].

The remarkable cave that bears this name was said to have a strange acoustic property. Prisoners who whispered to each other could be heard in a small chamber made for the tyrant Dionysus, ever suspicious. From this story arose the belief that the cave gives forth the echo which guides and tourists elicit. Another well-known showpiece is the Grotta dei Cordari, where for centuries ropemakers have worked in a cavern cut under the wall of the *latomia* [*below*], but if you want to enjoy the silence of this lush paradise I advise you to make for the other end, where there is only beauty and nothing worth seeing.

At the roadside, where the path to the Latomia di Santa Venera branches off—the quarry, by the way, tends to shed pieces of its walls and is frequently closed—is the little Norman chapel of San Nicolò and below it an ancient cistern which may at one time have been adapted by the Romans to flush their amphitheatre. This latter construction lies due south and is in a remarkable state of preservation, though not a thing of beauty. To the west, and opposite the entrance to the Latomia del Paradiso, is the Altar of Hieron II, of which only the plinth remains; but this alone is worth a look, for it is over 200 yards long and the bare blocks that remain give no idea of the grandeur of this monument or of the columns, portals and statues that adorned it. An altar on which 450 oxen could be sacrificed simultaneously to Zeus Eleutherios was an undertaking that was never equalled until the days of the Chicago stockyards.

The ruined church of S. Giovanni, sixth century but rebuilt by the Normans, lies on the left of the entrance to the catacombs. From outside, the remains of the west wall show a handsome rose window, and the south front a charming arcade built up of fourteenth-century fragments and incorporating even some Roman bits and pieces. Inside, you stand under the open sky and look down the generous nave, separated from its aisles by oblong piers joined by round arches. The pattern is that which we saw in the cathedral and may mean that the nave represents the *cella* of a temple, whose walls have been pierced by arches. An old tradition has it that the Temple of Bacchus stood here in Roman days, from which one can infer a previous Temple of Dionysus; the early Christians, like the Saracens after them, showed a predilection for housing their places of worship in those of their predecessors, combining sanctity with economy by pronouncing the necessary formulae of consecration. Behind you is the apse and here and there stumps of classical columns rise from their bases; Sladen even claims to have found the stylobate of the old temple, but I was unable to confirm this point or his claim to have seen a *krater* and other carved drinking emblems. In any case the building was certainly old, and was the official cathedral of Syracuse until Zosimus moved to the present site, prompted by the frequent Saracen raids which made Ortygia the only safe part of Syracuse. An open space across the road on the west side has been earmarked for a projected building with a height of 250 feet, to house the latest Madonna, the weeping one that we shall shortly see, and will undoubtedly spoil one of the quietest and most charming corners of Old Syracuse.

At the west end of the basilica a narrow stair leads down to the Crypt of Saint Marcian. Though each must form his own opinion of the authenticity of its various legends, there is no doubt that this tiny chapel represents one of the earliest surviving centres of Christian worship in the world. It is shaped, as was the tiny Byzantine chapel in the fields of Santa Croce di Camerina, to form a Greek cross, that is one with equal arms, of which three end in apses. The crossing lies between round arches, supported on low, sturdy piers built into the corners and bearing capitals with the volutes and egg-and-tongue moulding of classical style, in all probability taken from an older building; here and there the shafts of classical columns, apparently of jasper, chalcedony or green porphyry, but in reality moss-covered granite, have been revealed built into the thickness of the walls or used recumbent as building blocks, all evidence in favour of the existence of an earlier temple on this site. On the capitals, which are not all of the same pattern, are large dosserets in true Byzantine style, with various reliefs including representations of the Evangelists, but with texts in pre-Gothic Roman lettering and therefore probably dating from Norman times.

We know much of Saint Marcian's history from the writings of his disciple Peregrinus, and various features of the crypt conform with episodes he recounts. The Bishop was martyred under Gallienus and Valerian, so that the date of his death can be placed between the years 250 and 259; the granite column to which he was tied when martyred still stands here. His chair, a crumbling old wooden one, stands in an apse, and in the southeastern corner is a recess where one can see the tomb; it is characteristic of those of specially venerated saints and martyrs with its typical *fenestrella confessionis*, the window through which one can see the tomb chamber. Similar ones can be seen below the altar in many Italian cathedrals that house the bones of the most eminent, notably in the Basilica of Saint Peter in Rome. On all sides the graves of early Christians are huddled together, below ground level, in recesses and in various passages. Identification is somewhat complicated by the fact that the crypt was adapted from an underground Roman chamber, or hypogeum, and that the graves as well as the frescoes of earlier occupants are mixed with the later. The grouping of graves and the possible appropriation of a pagan necropolis are an exact copy of what has been found below the crypt of Saint Peter's in Rome. In both instances there is evidence that the early Christians believed in proximity to the relics of a martyr smoothing the path to salvation.

A legend—it cannot be more—states that Saint Peter himself was here in A.D. 44; as the New Testament does not even mention his sojourn in Rome, his visit to Syracuse must be discounted. Saint Paul, on the other hand, spent three days here, on the testimony of the Acts of the Apostles; the altar he is said to have used stands a few feet in front of Saint Marcian's tomb. In my first chapter I mentioned how the role of Castor and Pollux had been taken over, when pagan deities were converted to Christian saints, by Peter and Paul. Is there a clue to this in Acts xxviii, 11, where we read that the ship which brought Paul from Malta to Syracuse was the *Castor and Pollux*? A strange coincidence, seeing that it was as saviours from the sea that the saints took over from the Dioscuri.

More traces of the various users of the crypt can be found in the three entrances that survive; the earliest, dating from pagan times, is below floor level, the palaeo-Christian somewhat higher and at the opposite corner, while the one in use at present is Norman and, as we know, descends from ground level. Frescoes have also been attributed to different ages, from the traces remaining from the hypogeum in the north apse, through Byzantine to Benedictine. One of the rarest shows God the Father with the crucified Christ on His lap and the Holy Ghost, in the usual form of a dove, nestling in His beard.

Achradina preserves little of interest. Somewhere along the Via dell' Arsenale, on the eastern shore and facing Ortygia across the Little Harbour, are the remains of the great shipbuilding yards of Dionysus, with the rails on which the triremes were launched or hauled up for careening. Vestiges of a Byzantine bath house are near by and, as it is the only one surviving, some say it is the very one—the Baths of Daphne—where the Emperor Constans was murdered; the cynic may expect the discovery of the soap dish with which he was not slain at any moment. A public park now marks the site of the mainland agora, later the Roman forum; the only relic of it is a single broken column, smelling of urine, in a sheltered corner. A short distance from the Byzantine baths is the mean street with the gorgeous name of Via degli Orti di San Giorgio; at No. 11, in the year 1953, a mass-produced figure of the Virgin wept for five days. The Madonna appeared to a temporarily blind, pregnant woman, whose husband was a Communist. Her sight was restored as she prayed, and her gaze lighted on the weeping statue. The miracle has been confirmed; the population of Syracuse has grown and the Madonnina delle Lacrime is to be housed, as I have said, opposite the Church of San Giovanni.

The city's tutelary saint is Lucy, and a large church marks the site of her martyrdom; parts of it are Norman, subjected to considerable restoration. The sunken octagonal building next to the church was built to house her body, but this was removed to Constantinople in the eleventh century, when George Maniakes had conquered the eastern part of Sicily. The Fourth Crusade, successful in its main object of capturing Constantinople, appropriated for itself, by which is meant chiefly the Venetian contingent, a stupendous treasure, partly consisting of saints or parts of saints. Lucy, who was still in one piece and therefore probably of great value, was not restored to Syracuse, where her tomb is still empty, but lies in her own chapel in the Church of San Geremia in Venice.

16　*Outside Syracuse*

Leaving Syracuse, we go southward along the Via Elorina—note that this means the road to Helorus—and very shortly reach the so-called Roman Gymnasium, whose entrance has to be sought on the right of the road. Some of the local inhabitants call it the Baths of Diana, not to be confused with Daphne. It was neither a bath nor a gymnasium, but a small Roman temple backing on a theatre and thus providing a back drop. The ruins are fenced in and one may stroll there undisturbed, noting how the level of the ground water has risen to cover the lowest rows of seats and how a thicket of papyrus has gained a foothold to the south of the temple. Further on, the road crosses the swampy plain that surrounds most of the Great Harbour, scene of many fights during the Athenian siege. Along the water's edge, where salt pans are now being built, the soldiers lined up and tried to cheer their ships to victory on the day of the great catastrophe until, when the utter defeat of their navy had become apparent, in the words of Thucydides: "... now one impulse overpowered them all as they cried aloud and groaned in pain for what had happened, some going down to give help to the ships, some to guard what was left of their wall, while others (and these were now in the majority) began to think of themselves and how they could get away safe."

In the case of the latter it became obvious that the army was too sick to fight a pitched battle with any hope of victory. The Syracusans, reinforced by the Spartan Gylippus, profited by Nicias's infirmity of purpose. Relying on a soothsayer for instructions, he is said to have acted on a wrong interpretation of a lunar eclipse. Instead of going while there was still a chance of rescuing the last Athenian army, he waited for a month. His fleet was bottled up in the Great Harbour, defeated and then, when all hope could reasonably have been abandoned, Nicias ordered the army to retreat southward, leaving its crowded hospitals to a ruthless enemy. Sick and weary, the Athenians left their camp near the temple of Olympian Zeus and looked their last on the beautiful river that flows between banks of papyrus.

The fountain of Ciane can be visited by road, though many prefer to spend several hours being rowed across the harbour and up the river. The clearest water imaginable wells out among the papyrus plants, dragonflies hover and dart and grey mullet pursue a lazy, sinuous course among the water weeds. Paths follow the banks along the miles of papyrus—I have

151

discussed their origin elsewhere—and rustic bridges cross the clear, swiftly flowing river [*above*]. Further down, canes grow among the papyrus and poppies and yellow irises add their vivid colours. An ancient legend, supported by evidence that the fountain once formed part of a sanctuary, states that this, and not the Lake of Pergusa (see p. 183) was the site of the abduction of Persephone by Hades, god of the underworld. Her nymph Cyane, the name means "blue", wept so copiously that her tears filled the cleft through which her mistress had been abducted. I like the story and believe it; if a ten cent Madonna can weep, so can a nymph.

The fate of the Athenians, described so vividly by Thucydides, makes terrible reading. Again Nicias delayed retreating during the night when he could have negotiated the most difficult part of the route, this time because spies sent by the Syracusans made him believe that there were ambushes ahead that could only be detected by daylight. When he left on the second day the servants began to desert, the troops had to carry their own food, what there was of it, and Syracusan cavalry and light troops began to harass them. Native Siceliots were among them, and from what we can find in archaeological museums it is probable that leaden sling shot caused considerable losses; it may be that this weapon had been introduced a little while previously by the Balearic slingers in the Carthaginian army. Of all the pathetic sights and humiliations of a beaten army, the sailors who had now to travel overland were singled out for sympathy by the historian. They crossed the Anapo—this will have been above the source of the Ciane—and tried to break through inland to the high ground between Syracuse and Palazzolo Acreide; their enemies were ready for them, however, and after appalling losses the Athenians gave up the attempt to circle Syracuse and make for Catania, and decided to march south and seek a way through to Gela. Helorus was their first objective and its ruins, standing deserted by the seashore, are worth a visit. Much of the double wall has been uncovered, with a corner tower on a hill, overlooking the sandy beach. The main entrance between pylons can still be made out, as can traces of houses and wells.

But they were not to reach this temporary refuge. It is difficult to picture the countryside as it was at the time of the retreat; today it is one of the richest citrus areas in Sicily, and great plantations of oranges and lemons alternate with patches of almond and carob, usually fenced by a line of prickly pear. Not one of these existed in Sicily at the time of the retreat; there were olive trees in abundance and the rearguard under Demosthenes, 6,000 men in all, surrendered when trapped in a place where there were great numbers of olive trees that no doubt provided cover for the slingers. For the rest, I suspect that the ground was open, for the beaten army was continually subjected to cavalry attacks. The main force under Nicias battled on, tormented by constant attacks, presumably completing the square which the loss of Demosthenes had laid open, marching on until the next attack, fainting with heat and thirst, until they came to the River Assinarus, probably between the sea and where Noto now stands. Here all discipline broke down; abandoning defence the tortured men thronged into the river bed and began to slake their thirst. It mattered not that the enemy butchered the defenceless men; their rush stirred up the mud and they drank that too; their death stained the muddy river red and the survivors went on drinking that. The few that escaped the massacre were taken back to Syracuse and, with the six thousand of Demosthenes who had been promised their lives, were sent for ten weeks to the living death of the quarry. That is how one Greek democracy treated another.

I have kept the Castle of Euryalus to the end, for of all the marvels of Syracuse this is the greatest. The heights behind the theatre mark the coastal edge of a plateau, shaped like a wedge with its point at the south end; on this point was built the castle, which thus stood where the walls that crowned the sides of the plateau came together. Our road has the plateau of Epipolae, or "over the city", on its right and every now and then we can make out traces of the golden stone of the old wall. In places the low cliff has been used as a quarry and, at about two miles out of the city, a square piece of it has been left standing. If you climb the few yards needed to reach it from the road you will find that it is hollow and that what looks like a tomb recess now houses a farmer's implements. *"Niente tomba,"* he says vehemently, when

153

you try to explain that the builders of long ago must have left this portion of the cliff out of respect for the sanctity of its contents; all he can think of is the awful possibility of a department of antiquities, or some equally interfering body, taking over his tool-shed. Shortly after, you come to where an old wall, the main southward defence of the city, crosses the road; it is being restored with the original stones and interestingly enough contains an arched postern. It is often said that the Greeks did not know the arch; this is not the only example that they built, for another can be seen in the theatre of Segesta, and semicircular buttresses in the landward fortifications at Selinunte also show that building in curves was not beyond their powers.

I have often done the return journey on foot and each time there is something new to see or hear. The incredible labour of building a separate terrace for each olive tree gives you an insight into the poverty of the Sicilian peasant; calculate the hours it takes to build and to keep it in repair

and set these against the yield of olive oil per tree and its price, unrefined. You will abandon any ideas you may have had about retiring to Sicily to do a bit of quiet farming. I was resting on a wayside boulder one day when the music of a reed pipe made me look round; a shepherd boy kept repeating the same phrase in a minor key. I am not enough of a musician to tell whether it could have been an old Greek tune that he was piping; certainly it was not Arabic. Was it the Dorian or the Phrygian mode that the shepherds used? No matter. Close your eyes, breathe in the perfume of the wild sage and listen to Anchises on Mount Ida piping to his flock while Aphrodite considers how best she can tempt him to her arms and let him father Aeneas on her, Aeneas who carried him from burning Troy and buried him here in Sicily.

Eventually your road winds round the end of Epipolae and a short branch takes you to the clearing where the five towers of the keep lie straight across your path [below]. On your left is the museum. On your right high walls

surround the house of a Rothschild and, as though that famous name has to be justified down to the smallest detail, the glass that crowns the wall is of the most delicate quality; wine glasses at the Rothschilds', not ginger-beer bottles. Where you are standing was once the first of three fosses, and no road passed this way; on either side, amidst the undergrowth, you can see what was once a moat, deep enough to prevent the passage of hostile siege engines and yet near enough to the keep for the defenders to protect it with their own. It will be some time before you appreciate the lay-out of the fortress, and the guardian's demonstration on a map in the museum will be a help. Briefly, the wall and towers you are looking at guarded the tip of the wedge, while the way in, which had its own fortification, lay to your left.

The walls which surrounded Epipolae and joined it to the rest of Syracuse had the enormous circumference of eighteen miles and they, together with this immense and complicated castle, were put up in the years 402 to 397. The Athenian siege had nearly been successful when Epipolae fell to them and Dionysus, having taken over the government, determined that this would never happen again. You will remember that Dionysus became dictator only in face of the threat from the Carthaginians; with admirable method he therefore first ensured that Syracuse would remain impregnable and then, when sufficient had been built for this to be achieved, launched his counter-attack, culminating in the siege and capture of Motya, which we witnessed in the first chapter. Nor was it sheer aggressiveness on his part, for a short time before the Carthaginian navy had appeared in the Great Harbour and landed raiders, who destroyed the Temple of Demeter and Kore as well as the tomb of Gelon and Demarete; so long had their defeat at Himera rankled. One is often asked why this enormous area had to be protected and made into the largest fortified enclosure in the ancient world; the answer is that the inhabitants from the surrounding countryside, together with their flocks, could be accommodated here in case of attack and, by being almost self-supporting, reinforce the defenders without overstraining their reserves of food. Another question that always turns up is: "Who was Euryalus?" Like Mrs. Harris, "there's no such a person" and there never was; some prefer the interpretation "broad based", others "nail head"; whichever is right, the name Euryelos was applied originally to the place and not the castle, for it is mentioned by Thucydides, whose history deals with a time some years before the building of the latter. It is quite certain that the castle we see today was not that of Dionysus alone; various successors strengthened the defences of Syracuse and, especially under Hieron II, the Roman threat was countered by elaborate modifications, in which Archimedes probably played a leading part.

The three fosses form one of the most interesting complexes, reinforced as they are by a fourth on the brink of the escarpment to the south. The first one was almost certainly a moat; the others, with their intercommunicating system of tunnels, must have been dry. Under the fort, in fact, was a whole maze of chambers and passages, along which troops, including even horses, could be moved to any part of the defences. Rings have been found which are presumed to have been used for tethering horses, but the suggestion that cavalry used the tunnels is nugatory; it is far more likely that beasts of burden were used to carry away the rubbish that besiegers would tip in at night in an attempt to fill the fosse. One is continually amazed at the detail that remains. Here is the pier of a bridge [*below*], presumably connected with a sally-port and of a late date; there a system of caves with letters that no one can decipher chiselled in the walls—store rooms, it is thought. The

longest tunnel, over two hundred yards carved out of the rock, connects the third fosse with the main gate in a different part of the fortifications and actually runs outside the walls for a distance. It is an amazing piece of engineering, with oblong vents in the roof that are neatly closed with removeable stone slabs. Both of them show two steps carved in their side, and one can only presume that a wooden ladder could be placed here to allow troops to leave the tunnel at this point. This tunnel's north entrance is amusing in its modernity, for it forks into two parallel passages before emerging, the ancestor of the "In" and "Out" kitchen doors of a restaurant; at the point of bifurcation there is even a niche in the wall with a blackened hood, showing where the lamp stood that enabled the men to select the correct branch.

Upstairs, amid the tumbled blocks, stretches a carpet of wild flowers, yellow rue, white, scarlet and purple vetch, pink anemones, a rare asphodel and great patches of the nearly orange marigold of Sicily. Thistles too, and beware the giant with the yellow flower and five rows of murderous spines; perhaps clumps of them were originally planted by the Syracusans to discourage direct assault. The towers that block the approach from the point of the wedge are solid and were constructed, it is believed, at a later date, to support the catapults that could hurl their missiles as far as the moat. There is a mystery here, for one authority states that they were invented by a commission of engineers in Syracuse in 393 B.C. while we know that Dionysus used them five years earlier in the capture of Motya; obviously the father of all royal commissions. Parts of the south wall of the keep survive, and from here the fallen ramparts of Epipolae can still be traced until hidden by a fold in the ground. To the south lies the Great Harbour, guarded by Ortygia and Plemmyrion, and inland are the sites made famous by man's genius for construction and destruction alike; Thapsus and Pantalica, Megara Hyblaea, Xyphonia and Acrae. In a forgotten German classic, von Pernull and Rivela say: "The great rival of Athens, Carthage and Rome is no more, but the swamp of Syrako and the Fountain of Cyane and white-capped Etna gaze silently on changed times, even as they did on the frightful battles, the greatness and the beauty of the past."

17 *Taormina*

To the discerning traveller Taormina's supreme attraction is something unique: an ancient town that has been a holiday resort for foreigners for generations and retains its integrity, though precariously. For this we have to thank the government department which regulates these matters and for once to raise our hats to bureaucracy. Theirs is no mean achievement; the dozens of hotels, hundreds of curio vendors and thousands of visitors merge unobtrusively into this small, mediaeval town without more than one evidence of the frightful vulgarity that you would expect. The exception is the short street leading to the so-called Greek theatre, where the shopkeepers display their trash on the pavement, wheels of bells copied from those that used to signal the elevation of the Host, toy Sicilian carts and puppets and among a host of others, the carved, totem-like figures which are a speciality of this region. Though they represent religious figures they are far more evocative of an Indian tribe. I inquired as to their origin and was told that they were locally ascribed to Spanish influence. Is it possible that they were originally brought here by garrison troops who had served in the Spanish colonies of South America?

The popularity of Taormina possibly goes back to the Germans of the last century, who were enchanted with its romantic views and inspired by one of the few passable descriptions of scenery in Goethe's book. Artists of all nationalities settled here and frantically tried to commit to canvas the inexhaustible host of landscapes and subjects that surrounded them. By 1908 Sladen could write: "Taormina suffers from artists badly—they swarm, and have made models dear and independent . . ." Elsewhere he writes: "Taormina is flooded with Germans", and perhaps with a sly dig at their table manners in those days, "At some hotels they have separate tables for them." The inevitable result of the propinquity of wealthy visitors and handsome male models gave the place a bad name for a time, but the visit of the Kaiser, whose failings were of quite a different kind, restored its respectability.

Taormina's history is a sad one, a catalogue of sieges and destructions; so frequent were these, in fact, that their repetition becomes boring and we note only that it was considered to be the capital of Byzantine Sicily during the long-drawn-out struggle with the Moslems and was the last city to fall into their hands, in A.D. 902, whereupon all the inhabitants were slaughtered. Sixty years later the repopulated town revolted against its Moslem masters and again the inhabitants were punished, by confiscation of property and enslavement. A few years later another unsuccessful rebellion provoked the complete destruction of the city, and so the story goes on for centuries, until one wonders how even the slightest trace of the past could ever survive.

One of the wonders of Taormina is its indestructibility. The Greek theatre is Roman, but we can walk a few yards outside the Porta Messina to the north-east and come upon the old Temple of Zeus, whose stylobate and cella walls now masquerade as the Church of San Pancrazio after having for a time served as the home of Isis and Serapis, as has been confirmed, not only by inscriptions, but by the discovery of a statue of a priestess of Isis. Behind the old agora, which became the forum and now remains the only sizeable square in the town, is part of the Roman Odeon whose curved tiers of seats merge with the remains of an earlier Greek temple, possibly that of Apollo. In the forum, just outside the beautiful Corvaia Palace, stood the statue of Gaius Verres, until the indignant citizens overturned it in protest against his blatant infringement of their treaty rights. Between the forum and the Church of San Pancrazio the left side of the street consists of shop fronts in a series of arches, and only careful inspection will show you that

this is the old aqueduct, which finishes in an open cistern just inside the ancient walls, to be seen by climbing a narrow flight of stone steps. The ancient walls, by the way, are here made of irregular blocks of stone, cemented and combined with fragments of brick and tile, contrasting with the regular, narrow bricks of Roman remains [*left*]. They are possibly Saracen, more probably mediaeval. The portion of Roman wall that is shown is part of one of the world's few remaining Roman houses; I except, of course, the ground floors, sometimes with reconstructed upper storeys, excavated at Pompeii and Herculaneum. It is called the Zecca, originally the Arabic and now also the Italian word for "mint", and the discovery of a number of Greek coins in the vicinity seemed to confirm the authenticity of the name. I know the brothers whose family owns the house and they have told me that their grandfather, who was a blacksmith, spent a great deal of time excavating in the cellars, but without any benefit beyond that of the exercise involved. The house extends above the broken arch [*below*] into

which another entrance has been built, and the mounting-block of the last century and the telephone wires of this add a pleasing touch.

The theatre is of course the main attraction for the passing tourist and his coach usually takes him there after climbing the 700-odd feet from the coast road. To be sure, there was once a Greek theatre there, and a few inscribed blocks testify to this; but the Romans made a thorough job of adapting it to their taste and the disappearance of the first six rows of the auditorium is a sign that it was used for more deadly pursuits than the recitation of iambics. The view from the top of the reconstructed *cavea*, but not from the front seats that were occupied by the privileged—I will not labour the point—is stupendous. Over the roofs of the town the eye is held by the masses of *mascaruni* shrub, which make splashes of bronze as they change from spring green to summer red, and then follows the winding coastline to the promontory of Schisó, where the first Greek settlement in Sicily, that of Naxos, once stood.

I have left Etna to the last, though it is undoubtedly the chief feature of the landscape [*below*]. Crowned with snow during most of the year, and topped with its plume of smoke, it fills the right half of the background like an extra backdrop to the stage; during an eruption, and these are frequent enough, a dense black cloud can hide the view, while at night dull red

threads reveal the rivers of lava. Over eighty eruptions have been recorded in history, the first in 396 B.C., and the shape of the mountain changes continually as new hills are thrown up and old ones tumble back into the craters. Small wonder that the ancients peopled this ever active mountain with gods and demi-gods, whose voices still come booming across the plain when the daytime noises of the town are stilled.

People react differently to the towering walls and marble columns that form the *frons scaeni* of the theatre as reconstructed. Some feel that the bare brickwork compares unfavourably with the marble remains of Greek theatres; others rave about its rosy glow. It is likely that everything was covered with stucco in Roman days, possibly painted with varying designs and embellished with statues of emperors. Against this barrier the audience would enjoy the spectacle of men and animals being killed. One reason why so much of the theatre has been spared is that the Moslems used it as a residence for their emir, and that later the powerful families of Termes, Corvaia and (believe it or not) Zumbo were allowed to erect a palace in it; from these epochs in its history date the Sicilian names of *"Lu Palazcu"* and *"Lu Goliseu"*, which hardly require translating.

The Corvaia Palace, quite recently restored, is the most famous building in Taormina and one of the most beautiful in Sicily. A superb example of

fifteenth-century Gothic, it yet incorporates earlier elements, among others one of the rare Saracen survivors, the tower which faces you as you enter the spacious courtyard. Its interest is primarily for the antiquarian, for the portal at the head of the stairs and the biforate window are obviously of a later date, while the back wall is said to have belonged to a third or fourth century Roman structure. Today the great halls house offices connected with the modern science of tourism; time was when the Sicilian parliament met in the largest room to choose a king when the line of Peter of Aragón became extinct with the death of King Martin in 1410. The hall can be changed to a theatre and present the mediaeval dramas of the puppet theatre for foreigners [*Col. pl. VII(a)*], in greater comfort than is afforded the humbler audiences for whom the puppets are still living heroes and villains. One of the best of the travelling puppeteers is Signor Macri, of Acireale, a genial character and a fund of knowledge on the history of the Sicilian puppet theatre. His name, by the way, is Italianized Greek and there are Macris mentioned in Byzantine chronicles and others still living today. The *puparo*, as he is called, explained that though the legends he enacts are older, the puppet theatre first came to Sicily from Naples as recently as 1860. It had its vogue in Rome, too, at about that time, and strangely enough in Modena. I say strangely, because Modena cathedral is one of the few that preserve a tangible relic of the troubadour days, when the epics of Charlemagne's paladins and the Arthurian cycle followed the crusaders down to the heel of Italy; on the pebble mosaic floor of Otranto cathedral, for instance, one can see a crude portrayal of King Arthur.

That the puppet theatre found a home in Sicily is not surprising in view of the emphasis that the plays lay on fights between paladins and infidels; the traditional paintings on the Sicilian carts largely use the same themes. To the ordinary Sicilian the paladins are as real as today's cricketers and footballers are to our man in the street. If you climb the steepest summit of Agrigento and manage to get into the cathedral, which is under semi-permanent repair, you will find a shrivelled mummy in tunic and kirtle, under glass, about the only moveable object that has not been stored elsewhere. I asked one of the workmen if he knew whose remains these were; "Why, the paladin Brantomarte of course," he replied, raising his eyebrows at my ignorance. I think he meant the female warrior Bradamante. But if you want to know more about this fascinating side of Sicilian life and the tales which have come down through popular tradition, as well as through the works of Tasso and Ariosto, I recommend Guercio's fascinating book.

The main street of Taormina, the Corso Umberto I, is still the old Roman Via Valeria, which ran from Messina to Catania. It runs its level course from the Corvaia Palace to the Duomo, or cathedral, and then on to the Porta Catania. On the left you pass the abandoned church of the monastery of the Order of Saint Augustine, now a surprisingly well-stocked municipal library. The disestablishment of the monasteries was also responsible for the birth of Taormina's premier hotel, the San Domenico, in which the apprehensive visitor steps gingerly on priceless carpets between precious antiques. Field-Marshal Kesselring had the good taste to make it his headquarters in 1943, but his patronage resulted in a direct hit from one of our bombs; restoration is now complete, by which I mean that the hotel has been rebuilt. The Field-Marshal was sentenced to life imprisonment by a war crimes tribunal, but not, as you might think, for making a military target of the incomparable Taormina.

The Corso then passes through ancient gates in walls that lie athwart the narrow town, and every now and then offers glimpses of mediaeval streets, or rather staircases, to right and left. It takes you past antique shops owned by honest and knowledgeable men where you may make such outlandish finds as Corinthian drachmae and Parthian pennies and a cathedral that

preserves its thirteenth-century battlements. The charming square that fronts it, with its seventeenth-century fountain, marks the limit to which motor vehicles may proceed, except for a few mercifully short hours, and this wise regulation undoubtedly enhances one's enjoyment. Unharassed by the machine age, the stroller can admire mediaeval doorways and windows, the brasses and wrought iron that are displayed on almost every house front, and the trailing flowers that cling to the walls of the side streets. Climb the steep stairs on your right, opposite the cathedral, and you will come to the much restored version of the venerable fourteenth-century ruined abbey, the Badia Vecchia, with its Gothic twin windows, forked battlements and chessboard design of grey stone and black lava. A similar, but more pleasing building of this type will be found downhill, on your left, where the Palazzo Santo Stefano stands in its neglected garden, all the more beautiful for lack of a gardener's care, ablaze with wild flowers [*opposite*]. The cellar, whose entrance can just be seen in the photograph, is notable for the central granite column from which spring the Gothic arches that support the floors above; the interested traveller, with the help of a guide book, can disentangle the complicated plans of windows, mentally remove the present stairway and place it where once it made a majestic approach to the now blocked entrance portal and thus visualize the palace of the dukes of Santo Stefano in the days of their glory.

Above Taormina lies the Castello, popularly attributed to the Saracens, though it is obvious that some sort of fortress must have stood here, as protection and refuge, from earliest times. Al-Edrisi, the great Arab cartographer who lived at Roger II's court, mentions this as one of the most famous of ancient castles; the views from it are breath-taking on three sides and on the fourth the still, blue sea throws the domed sentry-box into sharp relief [*below*]. Even higher up the mountain is the old settlement of Mola,

with the remains of its castle, and some authorities identify it with the Greek acropolis of Mylae, which would make the castle we have just visited a mere outwork.

If we descend to the overworked coast road and turn south we first cross the stream of Santa Venera, another of Aphrodite's or Ashtaroth's descendants, which used to course along one side of the old colony of Naxos. The next river was called the Assinos and its god figured on some of the beautiful coins of Naxos; it is now called Alcantara, from the Arabic for bridge, and it is worth following it inland along the road which passes round the back of Etna. An old account mentions that the papyrus grew along its banks; exciting news, for it is generally accepted that the Ciane river is its only natural habitat in Europe apart, that is, from its presumed home along the Papireto river in Palermo in olden days. Today there is certainly no trace of it, but there is a kind of spruce along the banks of the Alcantara, whose upper branches sport grey-brown, feathery fronds that might have misled a casual observer. The surroundings of Etna are furrowed by lava streams, whose age can be guessed approximately by the vegetation they bear. It is natural that the ever-present danger should give rise to legends, so that Linguaglossa, on our left, owes its salvation to the miraculous staff of Saint Egidius, which halted the lava in the same way as did the veil of Saint Agatha of Catania. Ever since the days when Dionysus and Selenus were portrayed on the coins of Naxos the district, and especially the slopes of Etna, has been renowned for its wine. Amphorae found at Pompeii have TAUR painted on them, a guarantee that the wine they contained came from Tauromenium. It must indeed have been a quality product to compete with the wines of the nearer—too near—Vesuvius, whose well-known Lacrima Christi label used to be a warranty in the days when the appellation, as the French say, was controlled.

This is the way to the old, abandoned Byzantine churches near Malvagna and Castiglione di Sicilia, which I described in Chapter 6; there are, however, other points of interest along the road. Following it from Francavilla to Castiglione, we come to what is described in the guide books as a mediaeval bridge over the Alcantara. Before we get there though, there is a most interesting single-apsed Norman church at the roadside, the abandoned Church of San Nicola [*right*]. It is quite common for the smaller churches built by the Normans in the early days to have arrow slits instead of windows, as this one has, and in some examples, for instance the old Church of Commenda in Piazza Armerina, there are not only arrow slits, but an entrance halfway up the wall, suggesting the use of a removable stair or ladder, which could be pulled up in case of trouble and turn the church into a strongpoint. The same elevated doorway, without visible means of support, or rather access, can be seen in the side wall of the structure that was built over the Temple of Apollo in Syracuse and, as we know that the Normans built a church in the ruins, it may well represent

their main entrance. We are apt to forget that the first years of the Norman conquest must have been fraught with anxiety, for none could tell when a group of Saracens had really been pacified—witness the large-scale Moslem revolt under Frederick II over 150 years later—and the Byzantines, who still retained a part of their Apulian possessions, kept a covetous eye on Sicily too.

A hundred yards further and we come to the mediaeval bridge. Some say that it was originally Roman and took the road from Messina to Lilybaeum (Marsala) across the Alcantara at this point. One guide book, originally written before the last war, retains the bridge in its latest edition and another, whose author shows a trusting disposition, does the same. Both of them mention a ruined Byzantine church hard by on the further bank. Alas for simple faith! One arch of the bridge remains; the rest is a modern replacement of what the Germans blew up in 1943. And the Byzantine church? About 200 yards downstream, among the meandering trickles of the Alcantara, a level plinth can be found in the undergrowth. There are the foundations of a small apsed building and around it those of a precinct with stone gate posts, in one of which a hole has been drilled, as though to secure the thong which is still used to secure doors and gates. Samuel Butler, in fact, drew attention to an episode in the fourth book of the *Odyssey*, when the wraith of Penelope's sister Iphthime vanished through the thong-hole of the door; the door of his bedroom at the Hotel Centrale in Trapani, he said, was fastened in the same way. In the absence of a Byzantine church which once stood near the bridge one may suspect that its stones were used to rebuild the ruined bridge and that the plinth and the gate posts are all that is left of it.

A sight too often missed by visitors to Taormina is the Basilian monastery and Church of Saints Peter and Paul on the Fiumara d'Agrò. A *fiumara*, I should explain, is the broad, dry bed of a river, studded with gravel and boulders and impassable only when the river comes down in spate. To reach this one we turn north after descending to the coastal road from Taormina; a digression to the mediaeval village of Forza d'Agrò is recommended to lovers of the picturesque, but our own road turns west shortly after, at about eight miles from Taormina. On our right is the enormous, flat waste of the *fiumara*, with paths cleared through it here and there and an occasional figure washing clothes in the trickle that persists along the south side, or wandering between the stones, picking up firewood or other treasures that the flood may have left. After three and a half miles a huddle of buildings can be made out on the far side, at least half a mile away, and in the usually clear weather one can distinguish the pinkish mass of the church. A track across the *fiumara* takes you to this astonishing building with its typically Sicilian mixture of styles. The Basilian monks, belonging to an oriental order, had a long tradition; Saint Basil founded the first monastery in Asia Minor about halfway through the fourth century and the Rule of Saint Basil was widely adopted in other monasteries. Few people are told that the monasteries of Saint Benedict, of which Cassino became the head, were derived from the Basilians. Although the monks of Saint Basil followed the Greek ritual in Spain, they conformed to the Latin in Italy. When they first lived in Sicily under Byzantine rule, their foundations were most numerous on the east side; with the coming of the Moslems they found it impossible to stay, and after their departure their buildings were systematically destroyed. Hence the present ones, of which Saints Peter and Paul is the outstanding example, were built after the Normans had invited them to return, and a glance at the photographs [*opposite and overleaf*] shows Norman influence in the tri-apsidal east end (though the central apse has been squared on the outside) and the interlacing blind arcades on all four walls. A Greek inscription over the west door tells us that the church was built by Master Gerard the Frank in 1171, whom the monks possibly brought back with them after their exile in southern Italy.

It is almost impossible to attribute every feature to one or other style; the overall impression of the lofty nave with its crenellated roof is Norman; the interlacing arcades and the designs of contrasting stone and black lava are a Sicilian adaptation of Saracen features which in turn derive from the Byzantine; and the decorative brickwork, which gives the whole building a rosy glow, is purely Byzantine with its herring-bone courses. Eastern influence is again visible inside, where one can see the secondary cupola over the presbytery supported on many-tiered squinches. The old monastery

buildings have been converted and are now the residences of simple folk, but their interiors still show brickwork and arches similar to the interior of the church. Trees grow thickly round the little group of buildings and a clump of daisies outside the west porch seems to emit its own light. For once in a Mediterranean country, the birds make more noise than the humans and one can stay on undisturbed, admiring the play of colours as the eye travels from pumice to brick and from limestone to lava.

18 *Cefalù and Tindari*

Historically, Cefalù is one of the most interesting of Sicily's smaller towns. From the days of Cephaloedium, the headland shaped like a head, to Garibaldi—they still point out where he stood on the 5th July, 1862 and repeated his refrain of "Rome or Death"—Cefalù had its share in most of the island's events. A prehistoric house, archaic Greek walls and more than a mention in Cicero's prosecution of Verres show that the town was old and flourishing; from the last we gather that its high priest occupied an important and lucrative post, for one of the aspirants bribed Verres to decree the dropping from the calendar of sufficient days to ensure that the rival candidate was away at election time. Here Cicero produced another of his puns, alleging that this new astronomer based his calculations not so much on the heavens (*caeli*) as on the chased silverware (*caelati argenti*) with which he was bribed; our schoolmasters might have brightened our studies a little had they shown the lovable hypocrite, as Durant calls him, capable of producing forced witticisms as well as stodgy prose. Samuel Butler made much of the local name of Portazza, dialect for Portaccia or "wide gate", for Cefalù and claimed that this was merely the Homeric Telepylus brought up to date. He had the grace to label it a corrupt rendering, for the Telepylus of the Laestrygones meant "with gates far apart"; such are the scholars' diversions.

There is more than the usual trace of Moslem occupation in the language of the modern fisherman. *Ràys* is the Arabic equivalent (in Italian spelling) of *capo*, or head, and the skipper and mate, who are elsewhere called *capo* and *sottocapo* are here called *ràys* and *sottoràys*, just as the net (*rete*) is known here as *sciabica*, the Arabic *shabka*. Even an especially large olive tree is known in these parts as *saracinu*, as mentioned in Chapter 7. A popular local song tells of the girl whom the Caid orders to renounce her religion, and how her lover comforts her and says he will be faithful and help her. The city coat of arms, which you can see inlaid in the cobbled streets, consists of three fish and a circle which is by tradition a loaf of bread, of the shape usually baked by the Arabs.

For the tourist there is a simple algebraic formula: $x = y = z$, where x is Cefalù, y the cathedral and z the mosaic figure of Christ Pantocrator. Even on the day excursions from Palermo the coaches pull up in the square, the passengers are taken inside the cathedral and, having re-entered the vehicle, are whisked away again. The inevitable result is that the traveller, mention-

,ing on some future occasion that he has been to Sicily, is asked "Have you been to Cefalù", and on answering in the affirmative has only to say a word or two about the Pantocrator to be accepted as a discriminating sightseer. Though there is much more to Cefalù than the cathedral, therefore, we should at least begin our visit there, as it sits on its little eminence below the frowning cliff, presiding over its town.

The cathedral, you will be told, was founded in 1131 by Roger II, in fulfilment of a vow made while at sea during the height of a tempest. He promised the Lord that, if he should be vouchsafed a safe landfall, he would dedicate a church to His son at that spot; the storm-tossed sovereign came safely ashore at Cefalù, hence the cathedral. The story is not mentioned in contemporary sources, and historians, with the cynicism forced on them by the continual discovery of the truth, believe it to be untrue. The real reason for its erection, they say, was politico-religious: the previous year the vacant throne of Saint Peter caused a split in the College of Cardinals, one faction electing Innocent II and the other a member of the noble family of Pierleoni, Anacletus II, who had a Jewish grandfather. This Judaeo-Pontifex, as he was called, caused great scandal, and even the tolerant Saint Bernard said that "to the shame of Christ a man of Jewish origin was come to occupy the chair of St. Peter". But as Durant points out, the worthy saint was overlooking Peter's own origin. The only reigning sovereign to back Anacletus was Roger, and it was to persuade the ecclesiastical party to support him that Roger built the new cathedral for Anacletus to create a new bishopric at Cefalù. But Roger soon became reconciled with Innocent and Cefalù rapidly lost its importance, as experts have detected in comparing the type of work done on the cathedral before and after the reconciliation.

Between the original and not quite symmetrical Norman towers the upper part of the façade of 1240, by Panettera, rises behind the fifteenth-century porch, in the same way as subsequent additions adorn or disfigure the entrances to the cathedrals of Palermo and Monreale. Walking on to the waste land behind, one sees again the interlacing arches and colour contrasts of the apses so typical of the Siculo-Norman style. But few people are given time to admire these attractions before they are herded into the basilica, with its sixteen antique columns. Even then they are apt to miss the original timber roof and the traces of painting which are still visible, the lion font in the south aisle and the Madonna by Antonello Gagini. The mosaics are, it is true, of surpassing interest, not only for their intrinsic beauty but for the story they represent and for the fact that they are the parents of the far more elaborate ones that we saw in the Cappella Reale and in Monreale cathedral.

It was here that the first group of *calogeri*—I explained the word earlier —were put to work, and it is fitting that one of the mountains named after the mythical Saint Calogero should be in this district. The workmanship is typically Byzantine of the twelfth century, and obviously closely related to that of the Convent of Daphni, in Attica, whose mosaics, though some years

175

earlier, also date from the second golden age of Byzantine art. The Pantocrator at Cefalù rivals that of Daphni in sublime majesty, and if the message of those stern features and piercing eyes is lost on you, read the Latin elegiac couplet that surrounds the portrait:

Factus homo Factor hominis Factique redemptor
Judico corporeus, corpora, corda Deus.

"I, your God, your maker and redeemer, in human form judge your body and heart" is a loose translation of the dread message, and then, as though to reassure the sinner that all is not lost, He holds in His left hand the bilingual text: "I am the light of the world: he that followeth me shall not walk in darkness, but shall have the light of life." The centre of the apse is occupied by the Virgin, interestingly enough with her hands shoulder high, palms forward, in the *orans* or praying position of the ancient Greeks. The choice of supporting figures is also believed to throw light on the origin of the artists, for among the most important are the Saints Basilius, Chrysostomos and Gregory the Theologos, who were especially popular with the *calogeri* of Mount Athos.

In the vault immediately before the apse are the mythical hosts of Heaven, about which no two authorities seem to agree; the cherubim—here called in Greek lettering "*Ho hagios Cherubim*", thus combining a Greek singular with a Hebrew plural—vary from flying mammals to six-winged creatures that remind one of the unfinished picture in *Huckleberry Finn*, the painting of a woman with three pairs of arms, whose artist had died before she had time to delete those she liked least. Centuries later the cherubim would be amputated children's heads fitted with wings, or chubby cupids copied from Pompeian models, as in Serpotta's stuccoes, which I mentioned in Chapter 12. Many of the mosaics in the chancel are of later date and inferior quality, possibly as the result of employing cheap local labour after the reconciliation with Pope Innocent II. It is interesting to observe that the saints in the chancel have the Latin *Sanctus* when on the north wall and the Greek *Hagios* on the south. Saint Andrew, by the way, carries the normal type of cross, for the belief that he was martyred on the X or saltire cross arose later in the Middle Ages. The cloister, of which both Romanesque and Gothic elements survive, is being restored; the wise man will await the completion of this work before commenting on it.

The rock that towers over Cefalù has pre-Greek remains, including probably the megalithic house, and traces of polygonal wall masonry still mark the protected access to the sea of this, the original settlement. There is a cistern there too; some call it the Bath of Diana, others attribute it to the Saracens, who also left some fortifications. The little fishing harbour on the west side of the promontory shows traces of Greek wall incorporated into the huddle of houses and at least one converted bastion of later date. The best example of ancient Greek sea walls are those on the north coast of the promontory, but are not to be compared with such well preserved survivors as those of Tindari and Gela.

Here and there in the town examples of mediaeval architecture peep out, the Osterio Magno having an especially pleasing triforate window in severe Norman style. Opposite the cathedral the Via Mandralisca leads past the museum of that name, and from upstairs one can hear the semi-oriental cries of the itinerant vendors below. The museum was originally a private collection and somewhat varied, but contains something for almost everyone, ancient coins, pottery from the Lipari Islands, Arab jars, Byzantine panel paintings and the superb portrait of a man by Antonello da Messina, which is all that most visitors want to see. Even so, they will not have wasted their time. The Greek *krater*, or mixing bowl, which is also mentioned in the guide books, has a humorous representation of a purchaser and vendor of tunny-fish steaks. On the same floor as the museum the bibliophile will find an excellent library, in which some unexpected treasures turn up; one of them is a first edition of the history of the reigns of the two Norman Williams, written by Hugo Falcandus at about the end of the twelfth century and first published, as the title page states, in 1550 by Dupuys, "under the sign of the wild man" (the woodwose again!) in the Rue St. Jacques, Paris.

Our last call is near the lower end of the Via Madralisca, to where an underground public wash-house still functions in the Via Vittorio Emanuele. Two dozen pipes discharge a perfect cascade of clear, cold water into the rock-cut channels and past the stone blocks on which the kneeling women thump the clothes. Though usually simply termed "mediaeval", experts now place it as a Saracen structure, both from the ingenuity with which the water is conducted through the channels and from the fact that few European communities showed either the ability or the desire to instal elaborate premises for bathing or washing. Cleanliness is an integral part of Islam, and for that reason was frowned on by those who won back territories for the Cross; uncleanliness, they preached, was next to godliness, and their holy men and women implemented the abstract dogma by dripping lice as they walked. Last time I visited this rare and historic *lavatoio*, a mother and daughter, the latter aged five, were busy with their task [*Col. pl. VIII(b)*]; at other times I have seen residents filling their pails, some balancing them on their heads as they mounted the steps, and fishermen rinsing out their nets in the swiftly running water.

Tyndaris was a successful colony, and choosing the right side in the first Punic War continued to flourish. Ample records have survived to trace its placid history up to the time of the Arabs. Gregory the Great, at the end of the sixth century, congratulated the local bishop on the extraordinary fertility of the episcopalian livestock, and Byzantine fortifications attest the defences that were built against the Saracen raiders. But in 836, the year of the fall of Tyndaris, the records stop abruptly and the town ceased to exist; a village persisted there and presents the interesting features of outside staircases and outside ovens, apparently derived from the Arabs, and mentioned earlier in this book. Almost all memory of the classical town had been lost when Fagan, who had been unsuccessful at Selinunte in 1809, began to excavate here and laid bare some of the finest classical remains in Sicily. Along the hill top and up the slopes winds the ancient Greek wall of honey-coloured stone, whose blocks are so accurately hewn that mortar is unnecessary. The road winds past the dipylon gate and zig-zags up the hill past stretches of clean, smooth masonry that tempt the pilgrim to rest. For the majority of travellers here come to worship at the shrine of the Black Madonna in the sanctuary that stands where the acropolis once looked down a sheer 600 feet to the sea and sandbanks below. Black Madonnas are almost always alleged to have come from the east under their own power and certainly are Byzantine in origin. They are worshipped from Spain to Russia, and I have not found a satisfactory explanation of the popularity of their cult. Here in Sicily it might well be the subconscious memory of the

Black Demeter who was worshipped by the Sikels before ever the first Greek colonist arrived; did the same black goddess, with or without a horse's head or other totemistic attribute, flourish elsewhere along the shores of the Mediterranean? The answer is that she probably existed wherever man worshipped a fertility goddess. Diana of the Ephesians is shown, in Naples for instance, with hands, face and feet of black marble, and one can quote a list of male and female black pagan divinities ranging to ancient Egypt in the south and India in the east; there we can see not only a black Krishna in the arms of Devaki, an almost exact double of the black Infant Jesus at the top of the Scala Santa in Rome, but a Siva with three heads that brings us back to the three-headed Persephone once worshipped in Sicily.

The excavations are fenced off from the old village, but in one place the famous basilica [*page 64*], formerly confused with the gymnasium mentioned by Cicero, actually forms part of one of the cottages that preserves its North African style of outside oven [*page 80*]. The Greek theatre [*below*] is sufficiently impressive to rank with those of Syracuse and Segesta

but the outer walls of the city will always remain the finest monument to the first colony. The Romans rewarded the fidelity of what Cicero called the "*nobilissima civitas*" on many occasions, but especially when Scipio Africanus the Younger returned to it the statue of Mercury which had been carried off by the Carthaginians. The statue was appropriated by Verres, almost as a matter of course, and afforded Cicero one of his chief accusations in his prosecution. The remains of a few Roman houses are still visible and one of them keeps a portion of the *calidarium* of its private baths [*page 65*]; one can see quite plainly how the hot air circulated below the floor and rose in the wall pipes, an invention which superseded the steam bath made by pouring water on hot stones, and which was destined to be adopted by the Arabs and eventually become the Turkish *hamam*.

Having examined the Greek walls, gate and towers, and the Byzantine fortifications which later reinforced them, having walked from the basilica to the theatre, you are still left with one of Sicily's most inspiring views. On your left is the noble curve of the Bay of Patti, on the right the promontory of Milazzo, scene of so many fateful invasions and sieges; behind, the Nebrodi raise their craggy peaks in never-ending steps and before you lies the sea, studded with the Aeolian or Lipari Islands. Their origin is easy to guess, for the nearest is called Vulcano, while Stromboli, among the furthest, still sends up its smoky umbrella. The islands more properly belong to the province of the prehistorian and have yielded rich Stone Age finds that are displayed in a museum near the cathedral of Lipari Island. This is not to say that the islands are devoid of historical interest: Minoan and Mycenean ceramics and a Bronze Age village have been found on Panarea and today's tendency is for history to reach back well into the age of mythology.

As we look northward over this incomparable scene, we may remember some of the players who have passed across the stage. Odysseus perhaps, or certainly if we are to believe Samuel Butler; Hiero II, who won a great land battle against the Mamertines, and two years later, Duilius, who defeated the Carthaginian fleet here in 260 B.C. and earned the first Roman naval "triumph". Our own use of the word "rostrum" is derived from the speakers' platform in the Roman forum, first adorned by the beaks (*rostra*) of ships captured at Anzio in 338 B.C., and later by those won from the Carthaginians in this battle of Mylae. Augustus defeated Sextus Pompeius here in 36 B.C., and the Saracens in A.D. 866 defeated the first Christian attempt at reconquering Sicily. Richard Coeur-de-Lion passed here on his way to Messina and the Third Crusade, and no doubt Edward I would take this, the quickest route home from Acre, when he heard of his father's illness. The Angevins landed here at the second attempt during the War of the Vespers, and Milazzo was besieged several times during the War of the Spanish Succession, of which we hear at school of Marlborough's victories in Germany and the Lowlands, and nothing more. For eight months Admiral Byng blockaded the Spaniards in Milazzo during the War of the

Quadruple Alliance; was that, you will ask, the unfortunate Admiral who was shot for not defending Port Mahon against the French? No, John Byng was the son of the one who blockaded Milazzo and destroyed the Spanish fleet off Cape Pàssaro, and brother to Pattee Byng, whose journal tells us so much about a forgotten war. Away over Milazzo Nelson's fleet passed towards Messina in its pursuit of Napoleon, the latter having circled the western tip of Sicily to avoid detection. Garibaldi captured the town, thus securing strategic control of the whole of Sicily, on the 20th July, 1860, and on the same night Dumas found him asleep on the pavement with a saddle for a pillow. A week later he was to be seen in state in Milazzo castle, with the exotic and self-styled Countess Maria Martini Della Torre, who claimed to have been in the Crimea with Florence Nightingale; this is not as impossible as it sounds, when we remember that nurses recruited without Miss Nightingale's approval consisted of about half who were religious proselytizers and a remainder whose ambitions were divided between men and liquor. Milazzo today shows something immeasurably more important than fortresses and fleets, sieges and battles. The shore on the east side of the promontory glitters with acres of steel, chemical factories and refineries which are helping Sicily to share Italy's prosperity and which will bring the Sicilian more benefits than any steel-clad army of the past.

19 *The Navel of Sicily*

I have left Enna to the last because it is one of the high, inland towns of Sicily and therefore in every sense the culmination of a visit. Well over three thousand feet above sea level, it offers a pleasant summer climate and at any other time a welcome of biting winds that make the men wear their dark blue, hooded, Sicilian cloaks and the women their heavy, fringed shawls under which their young may shelter like chickens. But it is a noble old town, with a reputation for culture, and even if this were expressed solely in the kitchen, which it is not, your visit would be worth while. Until the city is included in the itinerary of conducted tours, the stranger will continue to enjoy true Sicilian hospitality and the best of food and wine in its unpretentious hotels.

Cicero is often alleged to have coined the term "navel of Sicily" for the town that was called Henna in his day; in fact, it was Callimachus who did so about two centuries earlier. But Cicero tells us the myth which made this town important in so concise a manner that I shall quote him: "It is an ancient belief . . . that the island of Sicily as a whole is sacred to Ceres* and Libera . . . They hold that these goddesses were born in Sicily: that corn was first brought to light in Sicilian soil; and that Libera, whom they also call Proserpina, was carried off from a wood near Henna, a place which, lying in the middle of the island, is known as the navel of Sicily." † I have purposely omitted unnecessary reference to the Sicans and Sikels, who have no place in a book that tries to link places with events, but it is known that both these pre-Greek peoples lived in Enna and we may be fairly sure that their fertility goddess was worshipped in the centre of her domain. For the fields of Enna offer a panorama of green or gold, according to the season, which covers the rolling hills as far as the eye can see. And when we remember that, in addition to the life-giving corn, wild flowers have rioted there since the days of the earliest narrator, we can only endorse the gratitude that they felt to the unknown powers who gave them such wealth. If we are to believe the ancients, the flowers of Henna were so abundant and so perfumed that it was impossible for hounds to follow their prey by scent across the scene of Persephone's abduction. It need hardly be added that she was gathering

* Demeter.
† Based on the Loeb Classical Library version.

flowers, and that it was Persephone to whom Milton referred when he wrote:

> *Herself, a fairer Flow'r, by gloomy Dis*
> *Was gathered.*

From which Addison drew the moral that unaccompanied young women should not go maying, except in sober and discreet company, for, he said, he had shown before how apt they were to trip in a flow'ry Meadow. The old spoilsport.

The Lake of Pergusa, alleged to mark the spot where the goddess was abducted, is neither dark nor gloomy, though writers think it should be. It is just uninteresting, unless you like watching water-skiing or listening to the scream of racing cars on the special circuit that keeps you from the edge of the lake. If the occasion arose again it is quite possible that Persephone would thumb a lift from Hades, or Pluto or Dis, to get away from the noise.

Everyone had their turn at Enna. Dionysus I, Agathocles and the Carthaginians under Hamilcar; the last name, by the way, I accidentally discovered to mean Father (*Abu*) of the King (*Melek*) of the City (*Kart*), in case anyone wonders why the Carthaginians thought up such silly names. And if it comes to that, Hannibal is only Punic for the Hebrew that gave us John. When the Romans captured it, the fortified town became Castrum Hennae, which was made into Kasr Yani by the Arabs, Castrojani by the Christians and so Castrogiovanni, the castle of an entirely mythical John, until 1927 when the imperial revival under Mussolini restored the ancient, euphonius and far more suitable name.

The city occupies the summit of a ridge that is usually compared to a horseshoe. At the eastern tip is a low rock in which a stair has been cut to enable the visitor to see the flat areas that have been chiselled out of the top, areas which are said to have held the foundations of the Temple of Demeter and Persephone. We can only suspect, as also at Eleusis, what dark mysteries were celebrated to ensure the recurrent fertility of the earth; here, as elsewhere, the myth of a horse-headed child, offspring of a god such as Poseidon disguised as a horse, was strongly established. Standing on this lonely rock one is irresistibly reminded of Erice, whose temple to the goddess of fertility also stood at the extreme tip of a plateau; both the beginning and the end of this book will therefore serve to remind us that the Sicilian's main concern today is the same as it has always been, the reproduction of man and beast and plant, and not the entertainment of tourists and the manufacture of machinery.

Next to the lonely rock, and large enough to bar access to it from the rest of the plateau, is the complex known as the Castle of Lombardy (*Castello di Lombardia*). Research has shown that it was a fortified area since earliest times and large enough to shelter the whole population in times of siege. In the first Punic War the Romans captured it, by treachery as was usually the

183

case with impregnable Enna, and in 214 B.C. the Roman governor Pinarius, hearing of a projected rising, lured the inhabitants into the theatre and had them massacred; we learn with satisfaction that he was later punished for this perfidy by the great Marcellus. A bronze statue outside the castle reminds us of the Slave Wars, and of the part played by the Syrian Eunus; it is strange that no Sicilian patriot could be found to symbolize the revolt against the tyranny of the more nearly related Romans. The Saracens captured it only by persuading a prisoner to turn renegade and show them an entrance through an aqueduct (some say a sewer), which they had to negotiate one by one. Of its recapture by the Normans I shall have more to say, but the castle was really put into shape by Frederick Hohenstaufen, who commemorated the strength and past heroism of the city by giving it the title *Inexpugnabile* and permitting the use of the double-headed eagle on the city arms. The story of this monster is a fascinating one and, like the custom of bestowing titles on cities, it has an oriental origin. Chaldaean, Hittite, Seljuk, Byzantine and thus appropriated by the western emperors who counted themselves the heirs of Rome, it eventually became a part of the coats of arms of the fallen dynasties of central Europe in our own century. Among its strange adventures, says Emile Mâle, "The Turks saw at Lepanto, on the ships of Don John d'Austria, the two-headed eagle that had once figured in their own flags—the ancient eagle of Chaldaea now turned against them." After the Hohenstaufens and the Angevins came other Fredericks, and those of Aragón numbered II and III used this castle as a summer residence and kept its defences in repair. But before the War of the Vespers, when the messengers rode with loose rein to every stronghold in Sicily to raise the country against the hated French, Enna had revolted against the Emperor Frederick's son and successor Manfred and killed the castellan. This was done at the Pope's instigation as part of the papal policy of weakening the Hohenstaufens and inviting Charles of Anjou to take their place; a noticeable feature of the Castle of Enna is the square merlons of towers and curtain walls, elsewhere in Italy the sign of the Guelphs, or papal party, while the forked merlons that are usual in Sicily are the badge of the Ghibellines, or Emperor's faction.

One may wander in pleasant loneliness through the acres of grass inside, splashed with the colours of poppies or marigolds; in summer a theatre occupies the first courtyard, below which are the vast and gloomy dungeons attributed, as usual, to the Arabs. Nearby are towers said to have belonged to the harem and the Garden of Roses, once the recreation ground of its inmates; further on is a great gate, through which the country folk, with livestock and provisions, could be admitted when danger threatened. In the third court is the great Pisan Tower in which the parliament of 1324 confirmed the dynasty of Aragón as kings of Trinacria. Standing on this lofty tower you may look around the partly ruined walls and at the five other towers that remain of an original twenty, and then out over one of the finest panoramas in the world, ranges of mountains leaning over the fertile valleys to the west, a glimpse of the Mediterranean to the north, Etna with its smoke-topped, glistening cone in the east, and everywhere a scattering of white hamlets along the roads and tracks that follow every fold in the pleated landscape, all converging on Enna. I doubt whether, even in Sicily, so many different masters have occupied a single fortress: Carthaginians, Greeks, Romans, rebel slaves, Byzantines, Arabs, the Lombard knights who joined in the Norman adventure and the Pisan knights who fought under Count Roger; Swabians and Angevins, Spaniards and Neapolitans, Garibaldians, Germans and British. The list becomes endless if you analyse what each occupant represented; the first probably included Berbers, Spaniards and Negroes, the last members from the whole Commonwealth.

Below the castle, where the Via Roma leads us into the city, are the traditional sites of the Roman theatre, the baths and a temple. A little way along a wall sign tells us that Cicero, while collecting evidence against Verres, stayed in a house that stood on the same spot; this is too non-committal for the inhabitants, who obligingly point out the very window through which Cicero addressed the applauding throng. The Duomo, strictly not a cathedral, towers up on our right and from the Piazza Mazzini we see the south door, of Chiaramontine style, of which a portion survived the disastrous fire of 1446. The triple apse, another part of the original structure, dating from 1307, is also visible through railings, and the outside angles between flat facets are often remarked on. I have heard it said that this central apse represents an original octagonal tower in the town palace of the Chiaramonti and that it was adapted to the Duomo when this great family declined at the end of the fourteenth century.

The interior arouses mixed feelings. The squat columns with Renaissance carving of bases and capitals—two of them by Gian Domenico Gagini, son of Antonello and hence grandson of Domenico—are of black alabaster, a peculiarly repulsive and greasy-looking material, but in the baptistery two of them are genuine antiques taken from some now forgotten temple. The font on the left, facing the altar, rests on a portion of a carved antique column, possibly from the Temple of Demeter and Persephone, and the iron

grill which closes the baptistery is said to have come from the Castle of Lombardy, where it closed the harem entrance during the days of Arab rule. The bell tower of 1600 is remarkable only for the sonorous tones of its inmates, which shout down the feeble efforts of the bells of the many smaller churches of Enna. No wonder that Cardinal Newman, lying sick in what primitive refuge the town of 1833 offered, hid his head under the bed-clothes to escape the noise. The populace, not to know that he was one day to become a cardinal of their own church, took this as an example of the

devil being tormented by the sounds of Christian worship. Holy Week is a good time to judge for yourself what Newman suffered, and at the same time to note that the processional costumes are Spanish in every detail. Behind the Duomo a short passage leads to the Belvedere and you will understand why Enna is often called the *Belvedere di Sicilia*. In front of you, three miles away, lies the densely packed town of Calascibetta on a hill that rises from the same plain as Enna [*below*]. There the Normans made their headquarters while they besieged the plateau on which we are standing, and

there, in the town built of golden-red stone, died Peter II of Aragón in 1342. In death he came nearer to greatness than in life, for his parsimonious successors put his remains on top of those of Frederick, *Stupor Mundi*, in his porphyry sarcophagus in Palermo; on its back you may still read how Peter's body was brought here from "Calataxibetta".

As you look down the almost precipitous slope at your feet you may wonder how besiegers ever found their way up; you will not be surprised that Euphemius, who originally summoned Saracen help, was killed in one of their numerous, fruitless assaults, and that the town fell only through the treachery mentioned above. The Normans were just as unsuccessful in capturing the town by direct assault, defended as it was by a powerful force under the Emir, Ibn Hamud. Count Roger, combining good fortune and shrewdness, first captured Agrigento and found that his prisoners included Ibn Hamud's wife and family. With these bargaining counters it was not long before a secret arrangement had been made with the Emir. The Arab agreed to Roger's terms, which were the surrender of the city and baptism as a Christian, but made the following provisos: first, the surrender must be preceded by a pre-arranged and if possible bloodless ambush; secondly, the Emir's family must be restored to him, and thirdly, he must be allowed to stay married to his wife, even though she fell within the degrees of kinship prohibited by the Catholic Church. Both fulfilled their undertakings and

Enna became a Norman town while Ibn Hamud retired to an estate in Calabria bestowed on him by Roger, with the title Baron of Camuto, not too big a jump from his old name.

If you now look carefully among the trées below, you might possibly make out the roofs of two small buildings standing close together. To get there you have to take the main road down the northern escarpment and, guided only by instinct, climb a goat track on your right. It is narrow and rough, strewn with boulders and the bones of an ox long dead, but after a short climb you find that it has given way to rock in which cart wheels have made deep tracks. This, apparently the old south entrance to the town, winds between a square building on your right [*opposite*] and a stone hut on your left; the square building is all that remains of the Byzantine tower that used to guard the approach to the city. The hut, now the living quarters of a smallholder, is the final degradation of a Norman chapel, the Chiesetta della Madonna di Ibn Hamud. For it was here that Ibn Hamud fulfilled his side of the bargain, entering as a Moslem and emerging as Baron Ruggero di Camuto, for he naturally took his godfather's name at baptism. It is difficult to see why such a historic building has been allowed to become so neglected and almost impossible to find, for no signpost guides the inquiring visitor; it is invisible from below and quite unremarkable from above [*below*]. Only close inspection shows the built up remains of what was the western

entrance [*opposite*] and the circular light above it; but the memory of one of Sicily's most interesting events, along with its authentic scene, has been forgotten by all but a few of Enna's inhabitants.

From the Belvedere it is only a step back to where the Via Roma opens into the Piazza Umberto, or del Municipio, where four plain monolithic, Doric columns, like those of Segesta, mark the façade of the Town Hall. Here, we may presume, the city was declared liberated in the name of Garibaldi in 1860; but not by one of the Thousand, not by one of the hero's lieutenants who had marched with him from Marsala to Salemi, to Calatafimi and Palermo and Milazzo. No, Enna was declared liberated by the correspondent of the London *Times*, the blond, adventuring, Hungarian Eber. In the same square is the Church of San Marco, attractive to lovers of Baroque, and notable for having been built on the ruins of the synagogue which, with its adjacent ghetto, stood here until 1492, in a district which is still unofficially called Judeca or Giudecca.

A few yards along the Via Roma brings us to the Piazza Balata, named from an Arabic word about which there is some doubt; it seems nearest to *Baldah*, town, and may have been a municipal centre under Moslem rule; at any rate there was a great block here, like a pulpit, whose presence was recorded up to the year 1800, on which slaves were exposed for sale by public auction. Here the Via Roma most unkindly doubles back on its tracks and eventually takes you south to the octagonal Tower of Frederick, a fruitful cause for learned disputes; its shape and general affinity to the Castel del Monte in Apulia would make it the work of Frederick Hohenstaufen, but it is probable that one or other of the Aragonese Fredericks also had a hand in restoring it.

This rugged, grey mass would make a fitting end to our tour, were it not for an echo of the more recent past in the Church of Spirito Santo in this neighbourhood. An old Byzantine foundation, fortified on the side that overhangs the precipice and with a watch tower now used for church bells, it has had many changes and, no doubt, seen many more. One of its renovations seems to have added a portal with a Latin inscription and the date 1817. Sladen, who is usually reliable, says: "The date does not prevent the hermit who shows you over the church pointing out the spot where Our Lady received the Annunciation and the stove at which she was cooking, and the nine green tiles on which she was standing. You are also shown the crown of thorns . . . At the back of the church is a vault in the rock where he shows you the niches in which the twelve apostles sat . . ." The stove, by the way, was in the style of the early nineteenth century A.D.

If this book has a lesson to impart, and God forbid that it should be intentional, it ought to be the old one that you should believe nothing you hear and only half of what you see. But how dull would life be if you followed this precept! Ashtaroth never took wing for Africa in the guise of a red dove; Odysseus never entered the cave of Cyclops and never had to

190

devise his own salvation and that of his companions; there was never an eclipse of the moon on the night when Nicias should have abandoned the siege of Syracuse; Archimedes never burnt the Roman ships with his concave mirror or lifted them up-ended with his grappling cranes; the Virgin Mary never wrote a letter in her own hand to the Messenians; Saint George never rode in the ranks of the Normans and the hounds of Saint Julian never chased the Saracens over the ramparts of Erice. The sixteen-year-old Conradin did not throw his glove from the scaffold a moment before his death, with the words "This for Peter"; the oxen that transported the Madonna of Custonaci did not lie down unbidden within sight of Erice and, as the Evil Eye does not exist, the horns that defend you from it must be put up in all those houses for quite a different reason. But you will never enjoy Sicily as I do unless you take the facts with a generous helping of legend; one day you too will hear the rumble of Hephaistos' voice, as he limps about in the bowels of Etna, bringing his own world to an end with those ugly inventions, automation and mechanization.

Bibliography

Adragna, V. *Erice*. Trapani: Antonio Vento, 1953.

Amari, M. *Storia dei Musulmani di Sicilia*. 3 Vols. Firenze: Le Monnier, 1872.

History of the War of the Sicilian Vespers. London: R. Bentley, 1850.

Anderson, M. D. *The Imagery of British Churches*. London: Murray, 1955.

Baker, T. *The Normans*. London: Cassell, 1966.

Barrett, D. *Aristophanes. The Frogs and other Plays*. London: Penguin Books, 1964.

Benjamin of Tudela. "Itinerary." *Jewish Quart. Rev.* XVII (old series), 688 (1905–6).

Boardman, J. *The Greeks Overseas*. London: Penguin Books, 1964.

Bottari, S. *La Cultura figurativa in Sicilia*. Messina: D'Anna, 1954.

Butler, S. *The Authoress of the Odyssey*. London: A. C. Fifield, 1897.

Pattee Byng's Journal. *Navy Rec. Soc.* Vol. 88, London, 1950.

Caico, L. *Sicilian Ways and Days*. London: John Long, 1910.

Cajori, F. *A History of Mathematics*. New York: Macmillan, 1924.

Cicero, M. T. *The Verrine Orations* (Loeb Classical Library). London: Heinemann, 1966.

Clementi, D. R. "Some unnoticed Aspects of the Emperor Henry VI's Conquest of the Norman Kingdom of Sicily." *Bull. John Rylands Libr.* *36*:328 (1953–4).

Cohn, N. *The Pursuit of the Millennium*. London: Secker & Warburg, 1957.

Consociazione turistica italiana. *Sicilia*, 4th ed. Milan, 1940.

Dahmus, J. *Seven Medieval Kings*. London: Allen & Unwin, 1967.

Davis, S. *The Decipherment of the Minoan Linear A and Pictographic Scripts*. Johannesburg: Witwatersrand Univ. Press, 1967.

Demus, O. *The Mosaics of Norman Sicily*. London: Routledge & Kegan Paul, 1950.

Durant, W. *The Age of Faith*. New York: Simon & Schuster, 1950.

Emel Esin. *Mecca the Blessed and Madinah the Radiant*. London: Elek, 1963.

Finley, M. I. *The Ancient Greeks*. London: Chatto & Windus, 1963.

Flacelière, R. *La Vie Quotidienne en Grèce au Siècle de Périclès*. Paris: Hachette, 1959.

Frazer, J. G. *The Golden Bough.* London: Macmillan, 1949 (abridged ed.).
Gatto, S. *Storia della Sicilia.* Siracusa: Ciranno, 1959.
Gentili, G. V. *Mosaics of Piazza Armerina.* Milan: Arti Grafiche Ricordi, 1964.
The Imperial Villa of Piazza Armerina. State Publn. (undated).
Goethe, J. W. von. *Tagebuch der Italienischen Reise.* Stuttgart: Kröner, 1941.
Gow, A. S. F. *J. Hellen. Stud. 54*:1 (1934).
Guercio, F. M. *Sicily.* London: Faber & Faber, 1938.
Guido, M. *Syracuse.* London: Parrish, 1958.
Harden, D. *The Phoenicians.* London: Thames & Hudson, 1962.
Herold, J. C. *Bonaparte in Egypt.* London: Hamish Hamilton, 1963.
Hill, G. F. *Historical Greek Coins.* London: Constable, 1906.
A Guide to the Department of Coins and Medals in the British Museum. 3rd ed. London, 1922.
Jamison, E. *Admiral Eugenius of Sicily.* London: Oxford Univ. Press, 1957.
Jenkins, K. *Coins of Greek Sicily.* London: British Museum, 1966.
Jones, H. Festing. *Diversions in Sicily.* London: Jonathan Cape, 1929.
Kantorowicz, E. *Frederick II.* New York: F. Ungar, 1931.
Li Gotti, E. *Il Teatro dei Puppi.* Firenze: Sansoni, 1953.
Maggiore, N. *Compendio della Storia di Sicilia.* Palermo, 1831.
Masson, G. *Frederick II of Hohenstaufen.* London: Secker & Warburg, 1957.
Nelson-Hood, A. *Sicilian Studies.* London: Allen & Unwin, 1915.
Norwich, J. J. *The Normans in the South.* London: Longmans, 1967.
Parris, J. *The Lion of Caprera.* London: Arthur Barker, 1962.
Rosselli, R. *Lord William Bentinck and the British Occupation of Sicily 1811–14.* Camb. Univ. Press, 1956.
Runciman, S. *The Sicilian Vespers.* Camb. Univ. Press, 1958.
Salinas, A. *Le Mura Fenice di Erice.* Rome: Salviucci, 1883.
Santangelo, M. *Taormina and its Environs.* Rome, 1959.
Scaturro, I. *Storia di Sicilia.* Rome: Raggio, 1950.
Schwartz, H. M. *Sicily.* London: Thames & Hudson, 1956.
Seltman, C. *Greek Coins.* London: Methuen, 1933.
Women in Antiquity. London: Pan Books, 1956.
Skipwith, G. H. "Ashtoreth, the goddess of the Zidonians." *Jewish Quart. Rev.* XVIII (old series), 715 (1905–6).
Sladen, D. *Sicily.* 2nd ed. London: Methuen, 1908.
Stoll, R. *Architecture and Sculpture in Early Britain.* London: Thames & Hudson, 1967.
Sutherland, C. H. V. *Gold.* London: Thames & Hudson, 1959.
Thucydides. *The Peloponnesian War.* trans. Rex Warner. London: Penguin Classics, 1954.

Tomeucci, L. *Storia di Sicilia*. Messina: Ferrara, 1955.

Von Pernull, H. and Rivela, A. *Siziliens antike Denkmäler*. Palermo: Virzì, 1905.

Woodhead, A. G. *The Greeks in the West*. London: Thames & Hudson, 1962.

Index

Entries in **bold** type are of major importance.
Entries in *italics* refer to illustrations.

EDGAR HOLLOWAY

0 5 10 15 20   40   60   80   100 MILES

AEOLIAN ISLANDS

T Y R R H E N I A N   S E A

*Cape San Vito
and Macari*

*M. Cofano and
Custonacci*

MONREALE

PALERMO

Milazzo

MESSINA

ITALY

Altavilla
Milicia

TINDARI

*Monastery of
SS. Peter & Paul*

ERICE

Montelepre

CEFALU

Francavilla &
Castiglione
di Sicilia

*Aegatian
Islands*

Trapani

Segesta

•Alcamo

Himera

•Calatafimi

Randazzo•

R. Alcantara

TAORMINA

MOTYA

•Salemi

Bronte•

Marsala

Mt. Etna

Castelvetrano

•Sperlinga

Adrano•

Mazara del Vallo

SELINUNTE (Selinous)

•Calascibetta

•Caltabellotta

•ENNA

•Sciacca

•Morgantina

•AGRIGENTO
(Acragas)

PIAZZA ARMERINA

•Augusta

R. Anapo

*M
E
D
I
T
E
R
R
A
N
E
A
N*

Gela

Palazzolo
Acreide

R. Ciane

SYRACUSE

*I
O
N
I
A
N
     S
E
A*

•Ragusa

R. Asinaro
(Assinarus)

S. Croce di
Camerina

•Modica

Cape Passaro

S E A